Terrific Toys You Can Make

Terrific Toys You Can Make

Joan E. D. Trill

Sterling Publishing Co., Inc.   New York

For Jenna, Jason and Dennis

With thanks to John and Derwyn

Edited by Carol Palmer

Library of Congress Cataloging-in-Publication Data
Trill, Joan E. D.
  Terrific toys you can make.
  Includes index.
  1. Wooden toy making. I. Title.
TT174.5.W6T75 1987   745.592   87-15904
ISBN 0-8069-6592-4 (pbk.)

   3   5   7   9 10 8 6 4 2

CONTENTS

COLOR SECTION FOLLOWS PAGE 64

INTRODUCTION

If you can cut a straight line, cut a curved line, measure and use a drill accurately, then you can make all the projects in this book. Even the most complex project begins with but a single cut!

It is not necessary to be a skilled woodworker, although you should have a basic knowledge of tools and techniques. There are no complicated joints—butt joints are most commonly used. Some projects use butt, dado and rabbet joints, with only one requiring mortise and tenon joints. As a woodwork teacher, woodworker and parent of young children, I wanted to create projects that are easy to make and fun to play with. I have had grade 8 students make some of the vehicle, bank and puzzle projects with relative ease in a short period of time.

Most of the projects can be made with hand tools. You will need a hand saw, coping saw, drill and bits, screwdrivers, and T-square (try-square). You will gain accuracy and save time if you have access to power tools such as a table saw, scroll saw or band saw, and drill press. If you have a router you can round the edges of the projects with a ¼″ corner-rounding bit to make them softer in appearance and easier on little hands—otherwise they must be sanded well. A power sander is a great finishing tool to have.

The Simple Toys on Wheels can be made in half an hour with only a coping saw and drill, while the Indoor Play Center takes the longest time to complete and power tools to provide the accuracy needed. I have included toy storage projects as well as toys because it seems easier to get children to put away their toys if they have lots of places to neatly store them.

The toys can be made even more terrific and special by customizing the basic designs found in this book: youngsters can have their own name painted or routed on; vehicles can be designed using the family cars for models; the Wood and Plexiglas Banks can be customized by using the outline of a computer for a computer whiz-kid, say, or using the outline of a car for those who want to save to buy their own. The addition of items such as specialty hardware, leather or cloth adds a nice personal touch. So give free rein to your imagination and knowledge of your children's interests and have fun adding your own specialized features to the basics given in the projects.

When starting out, first read all the instructions for a given project and study the photographs and illustrations which accompany the project.

When laying out and marking your wood, use a T-square (try-square) for accuracy. Remember to "measure twice, and cut once." Use a tape measure or metal rule to evenly space the screws to give a more attractive appearance. Locate the screws where they won't hit other screws. When assembling the toys the addition of washers under the screw heads adds a nice finishing touch and can be done at your discretion. I use washers whenever I use screw eyes or screw hooks, as in the Five-Car Train project.

Use a standard wood glue for indoor projects. Use an exterior glue such as epoxy or resorcinol for outdoor projects or the joints will fail.

I used sugar pine, mahogany and maple for most of the toys. Using pine or maple (light-colored woods) in combination with mahogany (a dark wood) results in some very attractive projects. For the furniture projects I used ¾" maple plywood. The back of the Indoor Play Center and Adjustable Toy Shelves can be made with ¼" plywood or hardboard, which is cheaper and easy to wallpaper. If you are going to paint instead of wallpaper the backs, I recommend you use plywood, as hardboard will absorb paint like a blotter and take five or six coats to paint. If your wood is not thick enough for a project, several pieces can be laminated (glued together) to yield a piece of the required thickness.

All surfaces should be well sanded and all edges rounded before any finish is applied.

Sand the project between finishing coats as well, for a silky finish. The projects may be finished with special oil finishes, varnish or paint. Whatever finish is chosen, it must be nontoxic, so check labels.

Although specific sizes of wheels are mentioned for projects, their size is not critical and you may well have to substitute sizes. Try to get wheels as close in size as possible to the recommended size. Wheels may be made using a hole saw, band saw or lathe. They may also be salvaged from old toys. If you look in the advertisements in most woodwork magazines you will usually find several ads for toy parts suppliers. These companies sell a great variety of items. I buy most of my wheels and they are well worth the cost.

You can most easily enlarge the patterns by using the enlargement mode of a copying machine. Copying machines can be found in libraries, offices, stationery stores and other stores as well. You can also draw a grid of 1" squares, then freehand copy the patterns on to the grid. If you want to make the toy even larger, copy it on to a 2" grid.

The finished toys can be given to pre-school groups, schools, hospitals, or youth groups, or included in Christmas hampers. They make great gifts for friends and relatives. There is an increasing market for well-built wooden toys and a woodworker may find toymaking to be profitable as well as pleasant. The completion of a project gives you the pleasure of working with wood and immeasurable joy as little arms squeeze around your neck in a warm "thank you."

METRIC EQUIVALENCY CHART

MM—MILLIMETRES   CM—CENTIMETRES

INCHES TO MILLIMETRES AND CENTIMETRES

INCHES	MM	CM	INCHES	CM	INCHES	CM
⅛	3	0.3	9	22.9	30	76.2
¼	6	0.6	10	25.4	31	78.7
⅜	10	1.0	11	27.9	32	81.3
½	13	1.3	12	30.5	33	83.8
⅝	16	1.6	13	33.0	34	86.4
¾	19	1.9	14	35.6	35	88.9
⅞	22	2.2	15	38.1	36	91.4
1	25	2.5	16	40.6	37	94.0
1¼	32	3.2	17	43.2	38	96.5
1½	38	3.8	18	45.7	39	99.1
1¾	44	4.4	19	48.3	40	101.6
2	51	5.1	20	50.8	41	104.1
2½	64	6.4	21	53.3	42	106.7
3	76	7.6	22	55.9	43	109.2
3½	89	8.9	23	58.4	44	111.8
4	102	10.2	24	61.0	45	114.3
4½	114	11.4	25	63.5	46	116.8
5	127	12.7	26	66.0	47	119.4
6	152	15.2	27	68.6	48	121.9
7	178	17.8	28	71.1	49	124.5
8	203	20.3	29	73.7	50	127.0

YARDS TO METRES

YARDS	METRES	YARDS	METRES	YARDS	METRES	YARDS	METRES	YARDS	METRES
⅛	0.11	2⅛	1.94	4⅛	3.77	6⅛	5.60	8⅛	7.43
¼	0.23	2¼	2.06	4¼	3.89	6¼	5.72	8¼	7.54
⅜	0.34	2⅜	2.17	4⅜	4.00	6⅜	5.83	8⅜	7.66
½	0.46	2½	2.29	4½	4.11	6½	5.94	8½	7.77
⅝	0.57	2⅝	2.40	4⅝	4.23	6⅝	6.06	8⅝	7.89
¾	0.69	2¾	2.51	4¾	4.34	6¾	6.17	8¾	8.00
⅞	0.80	2⅞	2.63	4⅞	4.46	6⅞	6.29	8⅞	8.12
1	0.91	3	2.74	5	4.57	7	6.40	9	8.23
1⅛	1.03	3⅛	2.86	5⅛	4.69	7⅛	6.52	9⅛	8.34
1¼	1.14	3¼	2.97	5¼	4.80	7¼	6.63	9¼	8.46
1⅜	1.26	3⅜	3.09	5⅜	4.91	7⅜	6.74	9⅜	8.57
1½	1.37	3½	3.20	5½	5.03	7½	6.86	9½	8.69
1⅝	1.49	3⅝	3.31	5⅝	5.14	7⅝	6.97	9⅝	8.80
1¾	1.60	3¾	3.43	5¾	5.26	7¾	7.09	9¾	8.92
1⅞	1.71	3⅞	3.54	5⅞	5.37	7⅞	7.20	9⅞	9.03
2	1.83	4	3.66	6	5.49	8	7.32	10	9.14

TRUCK FLEET

Wheels can be mounted in three basic ways. The first method uses dowel axles. Drill a hole all the way through the body of the project. (The hole should be large enough for the dowel to turn freely.) Insert the length of dowel and glue a wheel on each end, after placing a washer between each wheel and the body of the project. (The dowel ends should be grooved or crimped with pliers a bit to make indentations for the glue.) A little wax from an unlit candle rubbed on the dowel will allow it to turn easily.

The second method uses metal rods. Again, drill a hole all the way through the body of the project, which is large enough to allow the rod to turn freely. The rod is inserted and the wheels are mounted at each end using a palnut to hold them in place, after placing a washer between each wheel and the body of the project.

Third, since screw heads can look like hubcaps on wheeled projects, screw mounts can be used. Select a screw size that the wheels can turn loosely on. I usually use a #12 screw with a Robertson head. Try to use screws which are not threaded all the way to the head, as this produces extra wear on the wheels. Drill a hole from each side of the project to accommodate the screws you are using. Put a little wax on the screws so the wheels can turn smoothly. Place a washer between each wheel and the body of the vehicle.

When you have wheels mounted two on each end of an axle (as for the trucks) place a washer or washers between the wheels to prevent them from rubbing against each other.

Apply the finish to the projects and wheels *before* mounting the wheels—it's *much* easier.

In the photographs the coupling pin is glued into each cab, but I have changed this in the diagrams and instructions. The coupling pins are glued into the base of each trailer and the hole is left open in each of the cabs. This will make it easier for a youngster to join the trailers to the cabs.

Cab I

Illus. 1.

CUTTING LIST

Roof A	1	Maple	$3\frac{7}{8}'' \times 2\frac{1}{4}'' \times \frac{3}{8}''$
Front B	1	Maple	$3\frac{1}{8}'' \times 2'' \times \frac{3}{8}''$
Sides C	2	Maple	$2\frac{3}{4}'' \times 4'' \times \frac{3}{8}''$
Back D	1	Maple	$3\frac{1}{8}'' \times 4'' \times \frac{3}{8}''$
Bumper E	1	Mahogany	$2'' \times 5\frac{1}{4}'' \times \frac{3}{8}''$
Base F	1	Maple	$4\frac{1}{4}'' \times 8'' \times 1\frac{7}{8}''$
Stack Bottoms G	2	Dowel	$\frac{3}{4}''$ diam. $\times 2\frac{3}{4}''$ long
Stack Tops H	2	Dowel	$\frac{1}{2}''$ diam. $\times 3\frac{1}{4}''$ long
Seat I	1	Mahogany	$1\frac{1}{2}'' \times 3\frac{1}{8}'' \times 1\frac{1}{4}''$

You will also need:

#6 × ¾" roundhead screws—**19**
#6 × ¼" roundhead screws to mount headlights—**2**
¾" diam. finishing washers for headlights—**2**
Flat washers to go under the screws for the headlights and roof—**8**

6 large screws for axles with finishing washers **OR** 3 pieces of dowel for axles
2" wheels—**10**
Flat washers to go between the wheels and truck body

INSTRUCTIONS

1. Cut all pieces to finished size and shape (refer to Illus. 2–6).
2. Cut both wheel wells in the base (F) at 2¾″ diameter to ½″ in depth using a fly cutter or router (see Illus. 2 and 3).
3. Drill the coupling hole on top of base (F) ½″ deep with 9⁄16″ diameter centered and in 1¼″ from rear end of base.
4. Router the edges of the base (F) (except for the front which will butt against the bumper), with a ¼″ corner rounding bit.
5. The seat and stacks are screwed in place from the bottom of the base, so the next step is to drill holes for these screws (Illus. 3). First, drill two holes (J and K) 5⁄16″ in diameter, 1¼″ deep, centers to be 2⅛″ from the bumper and 1⅛″ from the side of the base (these are for the seat). Second, drill two holes (L and M) 5⁄16″ in diameter, 1¼″ deep, centers to be 3³⁄16″ from the bumper and 11⁄16″ from the side of the base (these are for the stacks). You now have the holes to countersink the screw heads—now drill through the remainder of the base in those four holes (J, K, L, and M) with a smaller bit to accept the type of screws you decide to use.
6. Drill the axle holes ⅜″ from the lower edge of the base to accommodate either screws or dowels (Illus. 2).
7. In the seat (I) drill two holes ⅞″ diameter and ½″ deep as in Illus. 6 to accommodate plastic play people.
8. In the bottom stacks (G) drill a ½″ diameter hole ½″ deep to fit the top stacks (H) into (Illus. 2).
9. In the top stacks (H) drill a ¼″ hole 1″ deep, then cut the tops at a 45° angle.

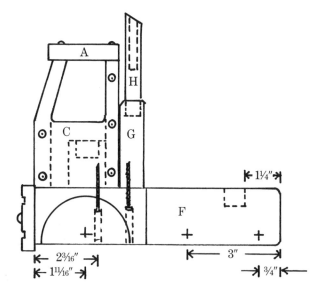

Illus. 2.   Cab I, side view

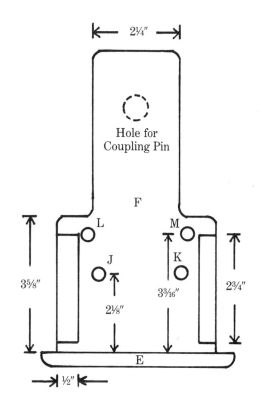

Illus. 3.   Cab I, base

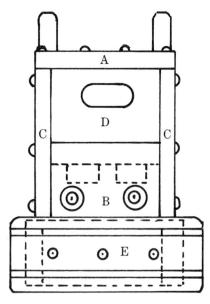

Illus. 4. Cab I, front view

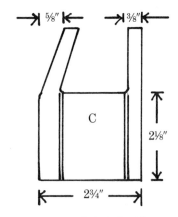

Illus. 5. Cab I, left side

10. In the sides (C) cut grooves ⅛″ wide and ⅛″ deep to look like doors (Illus. 5).
11. In the bumper (E) cut grooves ⅛″ wide and ¹⁄₁₆″ deep for a more finished look (Illus. 4).
12. In the front (B) drill two holes for the screw and washer "headlights" (Illus. 4).
13. Sand off all sharp edges; then before you begin assembly put all the pieces together to check their fit.
14. Glue and screw the seat (I) to the base (F) through holes J and K. Center the seat and have front of seat set back 1⅛″ from the front edge of the base (Illus. 6).
15. Glue and screw the back (D) to the base (F) and seat (I).
16. Glue and screw the doors to the base, seat, and back with butt joints.
17. Glue and screw the front (B) to the sides with butt joints.
18. Glue and screw the roof (A) to the back and sides with butt joints.
19. Glue and screw the bumper (E) to the front.
20. Glue the top stacks to the bottom stacks, then screw the stacks in place immediately behind the cab through holes L and M.
21. Mount two 2″ wheels on each side of the rear axles and one on each side of the front axle, placing flat washers between the wheels and the truck body.

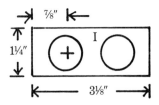

Illus. 6. Cab I seat, top view

CAB II

Illus. 7.

CUTTING LIST

Seat A	1	Mahogany	3⅛" × 1¼" × 1½"
Base B	1	Maple	10" × 4¼" × 1⅞"
Motor Housing C	1	Maple	2⅛" × 3⅞" × 2¾"
Cab Sides D	2	Mahogany	4" × 2⅜" × ⅜"
Cab Back E	1	Mahogany	4" × 3⅛" × ⅜"
Roof F	1	Maple	2¼" × 3⅞" × ⅜"
Wheel Housing G	2	Maple	2¾" × 1¼" × 1¾"
Bumper H	1	Mahogany	5¼" × 2" × ⅜"
Stack Bottoms I	2	Dowel	¾" diam. × 2¾" long
Stack Tops J	2	Dowel	½" diam. × 3¼" long

You will also need:

#6 × ¾" roundhead screws to assemble the sides and top—**12**

#6 × ¼" roundhead screws to mount the headlights—**2**

¾" finishing washers for headlights—**2**

Flat washers to go under the heads of the #6 screws—**12**

Six #12 × 2" screws for the axles **OR** 3 pieces of dowel or metal rod

2" wheels—**10**

INSTRUCTIONS

1. Cut all pieces to finished size (refer to Illus. 8–15).
2. In the base (B) cut the wheel wells with a fly cutter or router, *then* shape the motor housing (C) (Illus. 8, 9, and 10). Shape the wheel housings (G) (Illus. 12, 13, and 14), cab sides (D) (Illus. 15) and cut the rear-view window in the cab back (E) (Illus. 9).
3. Drill the holes in the cab seat (A) ⅞″ in diameter and ½″ deep (Illus. 11). These will accommodate small plastic play people.
4. Drill a ½″ diameter hole 1″ deep into the bottom section of each exhaust stack (I). Drill a ¼″ diameter hole 1″ deep into the top section of each exhaust stack (J), then angle the top of these at 45°. Glue the top section into the bottom section (Illus. 8).
5. The seat, stacks and motor housing are screwed in place from the bottom of the base, so the next step is to drill holes for these screws (Illus. 10). First, drill two holes (J and K) 5⁄16″ in diameter, 1¼″ deep for the seat. Second, drill three 5⁄16″ diameter holes (L, M, and N) 1¼″ deep for the motor housing. Third, drill two holes (O and P) 5⁄16″ diameter, 1¼″ deep for the stacks. You now have the holes to countersink the screw heads—next drill through the remainder of the base in these holes to accept the type of screws you decide to use.

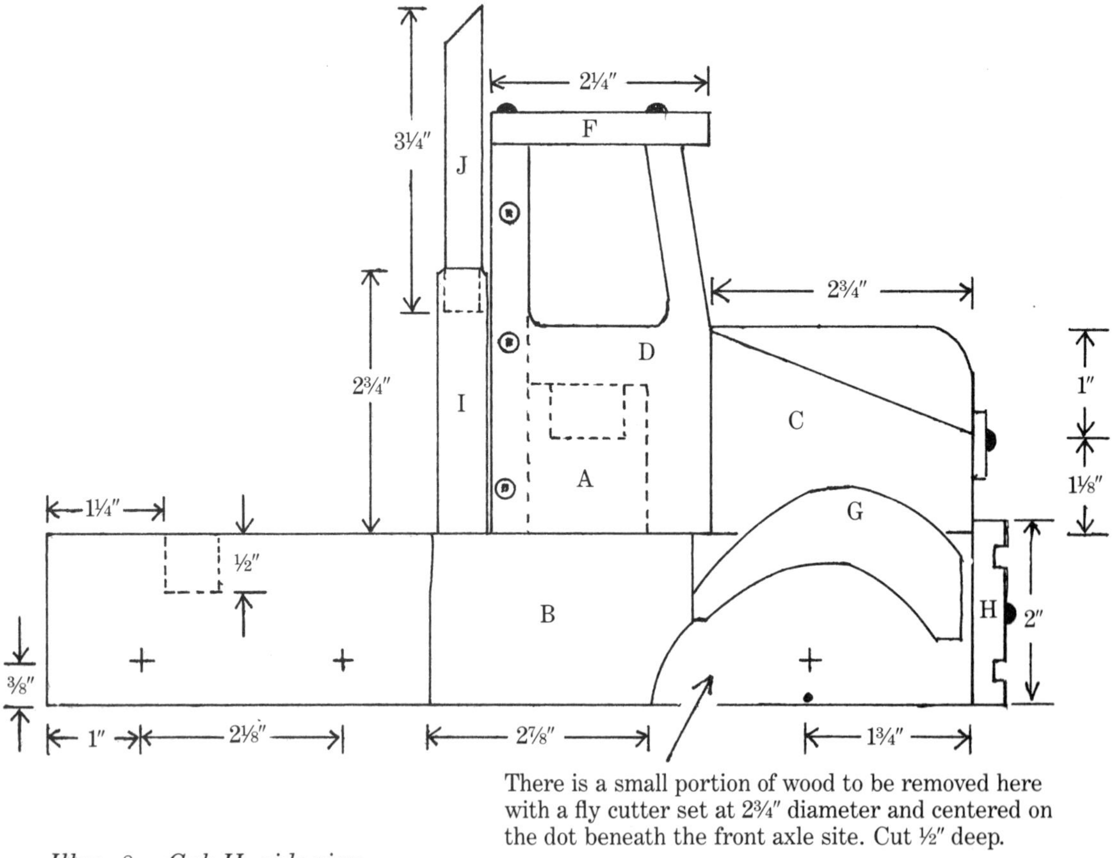

2¼″
F
3¼″
J
2¾″
D
2¾″
I
C
1″
A
1⅛″
G
1¼″
½″
B
H
2″
⅜″
1″
2⅛″
2⅞″
1¾″
There is a small portion of wood to be removed here with a fly cutter set at 2¾″ diameter and centered on the dot beneath the front axle site. Cut ½″ deep.

Illus. 8. Cab II, side view

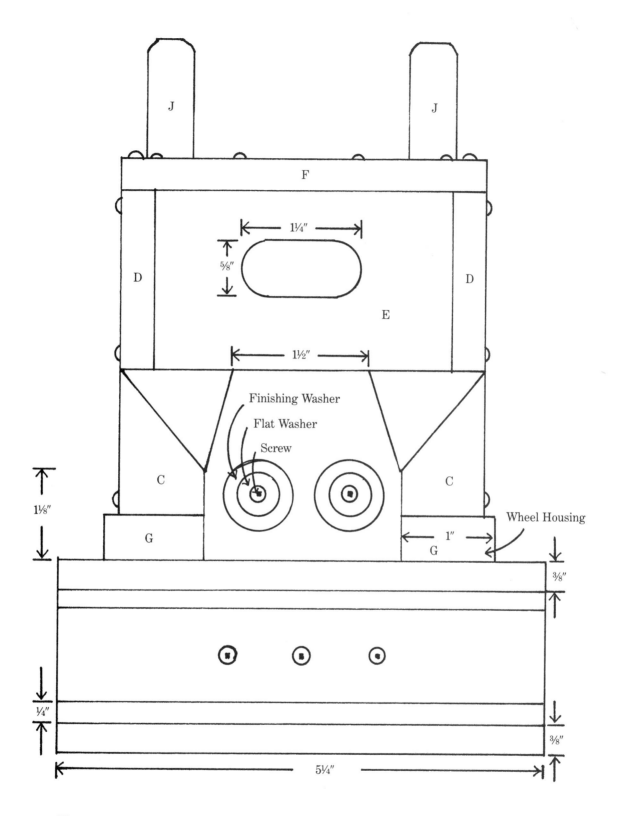

Illus. 9.   Cab II, front view

19

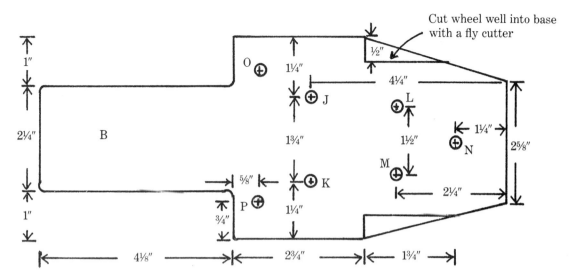

Illus. 10. Cab II, bottom of base showing dimensions and screw locations.

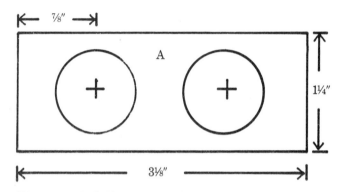

Illus. 11. Cab II seat, top view

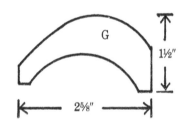

Illus. 12. Cab II wheel wells, side view

6. In the bumper (H) cut grooves ⅛″ wide and 1⁄16″ deep for a more finished look (Illus. 8).

7. In the front of the motor housing (C) drill two holes for the screw and washer "headlights" (Illus. 9).

8. Place all the pieces together with no glue or screws to check their fit. Using glue and recessed screws from the bottom of the base, attach the motor housing, then the seat, to the base. Attach the cab back and sides around the seat

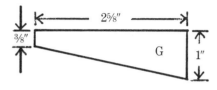

Illus. 13.   Cab II, left wheel well, top view

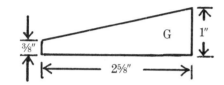

Illus. 14.   Cab II, right wheel well, top view

using glue and screws. Add the roof using screws and glue—a flat washer under the screw heads adds an interesting touch. Using glue and recessed screws attach the exhaust stacks behind the cab. Add the bumper with glue and screws.

9. Drill axle holes (Illus. 8). Wheels can be mounted on dowels which turn loosely through the base, or on screws. The size of the axle holes will be determined by the method you choose. In either case place a flat washer between the heel and truck body.

10. Finish as desired.

11. Mount the wheels and you're ready to roll.

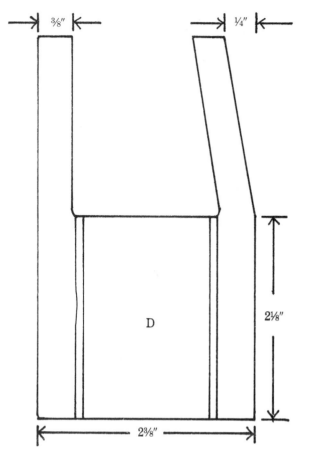

Illus. 15.   Cab II door, right side

Transport Trailer

Illus. 16.

CUTTING LIST

Front A	1	Plywood	3⅞″ × 5⅝″ × ¼″
Sides B	2	Plywood	15½″ × 5⅝″ × ¼″
Roof C	2	Plywood	13½″ × 2¹¹⁄₁₆″ × ¼″
Roof D	1	Plywood	14¹¹⁄₁₆″ × 4⅜″ × ¼″
Roof E	1	Plywood	¹³⁄₁₆″ × 4⅜″ × ¼″
Base F	1	Pine	15¼″ × 3⅞″ × ¾″
Wheel Block G	1	Pine	4½″ × 2½″ × 1⅞″
Stands H	2	Mahogany	2½″ × 1″ × ¼″
Dowel I	1	Dowel	⅜″ diam. × 5⅛″ long
Doors J	2	Pine	4¹³⁄₁₆″ × 1⅞″ × ⁵⁄₁₆″
Door Latch K	1	Mahogany	2″ × ⁷⁄₁₆″ × ¼″
Coupling Pin L	1	Dowel	½″ diam. × 1⅛″ long
Corner Reinforcers	2		14¾″ × ½″ × ½″
Corner Reinforcers	4		4⁵⁄₁₆″ × ½″ × ½″
Corner Reinforcers	2		2¾″ × ½″ × ½″

You will also need: #6 × ¾″ screws, finishing nails, eight 2″ wheels, two ⁷⁄₁₆″ screw eyes and axles.

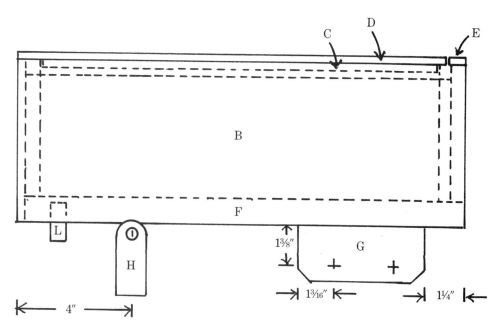

Illus. 17. Transport Trailer, side view

INSTRUCTIONS

1. Cut all pieces to finished size and shape (see Illus. 17–21).
2. Drill axle holes in the wheel block (G) to accept either screws or dowels. Cut the bottom corners at 45° (Illus. 17).
3. Drill the coupling pin hole on the bottom of the base (F) ½″ in diameter, ½″ deep, 1″ from the front end and centered. Drill two holes 4″ from the front edge and ½″ from the sides to accept ⁷⁄₁₆″ screw eyes.
4. In each stand (H) drill a ⅜″ diameter hole centered and down ⅜″ from the top to fit the dowel (I) into. Round off the top corners as in Illus. 17.
5. Glue and/or screw the wheel block (G) to the base (F) centered and 1¼″ in from the rear end of the base (Illus. 17). See Illus. 19.
6. Glue and/or screw the coupling pin (L) in place.

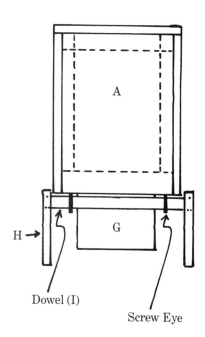

Illus. 18. Transport Trailer, front view

23

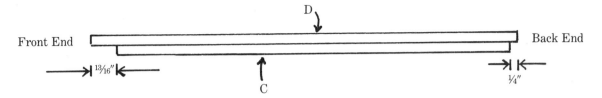

D

Front End   Back End

13⁄16″

C

¼″

Illus. 19.   Transport Trailer roof, side view

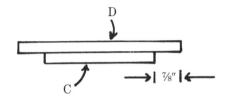

D

C

⅞″

Illus. 20.   Transport Trailer roof, end view

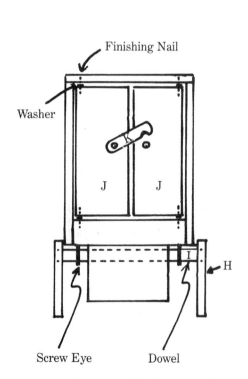

Finishing Nail

Washer

J   J

H

Screw Eye   Dowel

Illus. 21.   Transport Trailer, rear view

Illus. 22.   Detail of rear door

Illus. 23.   Transport Trailer showing lift-off top

Illus. 24.   Detail of wheel stands and wheel block

Illus. 25.   Detail of Dowel I

7. Glue and screw the corner reinforcers to the top edges of the sides (B); begin ¼″ in from the front end to allow for the fitting in of the front piece. (The space at the rear is to allow for the doors.) Attach the sides to the base.

8. Glue and screw the front (A) to the base (F) using corner reinforcers for added strength in the left and right corners and along the top edge (Illus. 18).

9. Attach the corner reinforcers at the rear on the left and right sides ½″ in from the end. Attach the top reinforcer.

10. Glue and screw the small roof pieces (E) at the back edge of the trailer (Illus. 17).

11. Mount the doors. Use finishing nails as hinges for the doors to pivot on (see Illus. 22). Place nails through small washers between the door and the truck body. The outer edges of the doors may have to be rounded to allow clearance for opening and closing. Screw the door latch and put a screw on the right-hand side for the latch to slip into (Illus. 21).

12. Screw the ⁷⁄₁₆″ screw eyes into their holes. Check that the dowel will be a tight fit. Put the dowel (I) through the screw eyes and attach both stands (H) with glue and a small finishing nail (see Illus. 25).

13. Glue roof piece (C) to the bottom of roof piece (D) to make a lift-off roof (Illus. 19 and 20).

14. Finish the wheels and truck; then mount two 2″ wheel on each side of the axles.

15. Lettering may be applied with rub-on lettering, or can be painted on.

Stock Trailer

Illus. 26.

CUTTING LIST

				L	W	T
Roof A	1	Plywood	$15\frac{1}{2}'' \times 4\frac{1}{4}'' \times \frac{1}{4}''$			
Front B	1	Plywood	$5\frac{7}{8}'' \times 4\frac{1}{4}'' \times \frac{1}{4}''$			
Base C	1	Pine	$15\frac{1}{4}'' \times 4'' \times \frac{3}{4}''$			
Slats D	12	Mahogany	$15\frac{1}{4}'' \times \frac{5}{8}'' \times \frac{3}{16}''$			
Vertical Supports E	6	Mahogany	$5\frac{1}{8}'' \times \frac{1}{2}'' \times \frac{3}{4}''$			
Glue Blocks F	10	Scrap	$\frac{1}{2}''$ thick triangles $1\frac{1}{4}'' \times 1\frac{1}{4}'' \times 1\frac{13}{16}''$			
Door G	1	Pine	$5\frac{3}{4}'' \times 2\frac{3}{4}'' \times \frac{7}{16}''$			
Wheel Block H	1	Pine	$4\frac{1}{2}'' \times 2\frac{1}{2}'' \times 1\frac{7}{8}''$			
Stand I	2	Mahogany	$2\frac{1}{2}'' \times 1'' \times \frac{1}{4}''$			
Dowel J	1	Dowel	$\frac{3}{8}''$ diam. $\times 5\frac{1}{8}''$ long			
Coupling Pin K	1	Dowel	$\frac{1}{2}''$ diam. $\times 1\frac{1}{8}''$ long			
Door Stop L	1	Mahogany	$2\frac{3}{4}'' \times \frac{1}{2}'' \times \frac{1}{4}''$			

You will also need: *two $\frac{7}{16}''$ screw eyes, screws, axles, two screen fasteners, and eight 2'' wheels.*

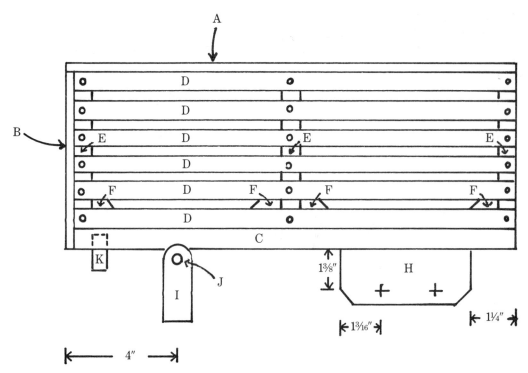

Illus. 27.   Stock Trailer, side view

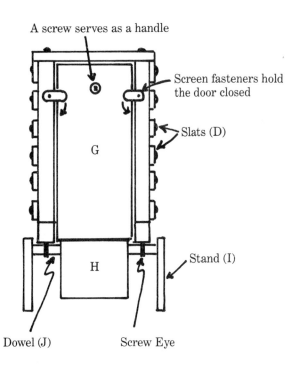

A screw serves as a handle

Screen fasteners hold
the door closed

Slats (D)

Stand (I)

Dowel (J)   Screw Eye

Illus. 28.   Stock Trailer, rear view

INSTRUCTIONS

1. For the slats (D) cut a piece of mahogany to length, then rip twelve slats.
2. Cut the stands (I) to size and shape, then drill holes ⅜″ diameter centered and ⅜″ from the top edge to fit the dowel (J) into (Illus. 27).
3. Cut the remaining pieces to size and shape (refer to Illus. 27–31).
4. In the base (C) drill two holes 4″ from the front edge and ½″ in from the sides to accept the ⁷⁄₁₆″ screw eyes. Drill the coupling pin hole with ½″ diameter, ½″ deep 1″ from the front end and centered. Cut the door notch at the rear as per Illus. 31.
5. In the wheel block (H) drill the axle holes and cut the bottom corners at 45° (Illus. 27).

6. Cut grooves in the door (G) to provide "secure footing" for animals (Illus. 29).

7. Glue and screw the wheel block (H) to the base (C).

8. Glue the coupling pin (K) in place (Illus. 27).

9. Glue and screw six slats per side to three vertical supports (E), spacing them evenly. (#6 × ¾″ round head screws work well.) Attach the assembled sides to the base using glue and screws coming up from the base into each of the vertical supports. Reinforce the verticals with triangular glue blocks (F) (Illus. 30).

10. Glue and screw the roof (A) to the sides.

11. Glue and screw the front to the base and vertical supports.

12. Mount the door-loading ramp using a screw or nail on each side to act as a pivot point. The bottom of the door should be rounded (Illus. 29) to allow sufficient clearance. Place a small washer between the door and base. Mount screen fasteners or another device to hold the door in the closed position. Attach a screw to the door centered and 1″ down from the top to act as a door pull. Glue a strip of wood on the underside of the roof to act as a door stop.

13. Screw the screw eyes in place. Run the dowel (J) through the screw eyes and attach both stands—secure the dowel with glue and a small finishing nail. The dowel should turn very snugly in the screw eyes.

14. Mount two 2″ wheels on each side of the axles.

15. Load 'em up and head 'em out!

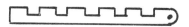

Illus. 29.   Stock Trailer door (G), side view

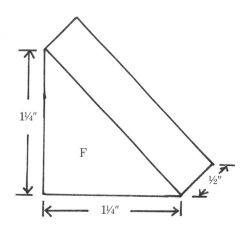

Illus. 30.   Glue block detail

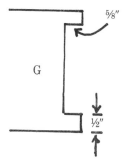

Illus. 31.   Notch for door (G) at rear end of base

Logging Trailer

Illus. 32.

CUTTING LIST

Base A	*1*	*Pine or Mahogany*	*15½″ × 4¼″ × ¾″*
Wheel Block B	*1*	*Pine*	*4¼″ × 2½″ × 1⅞″*
Stands C	*2*	*Mahogany*	*2½″ × 1″ × ¼″*
Dowel D	*1*	*Dowel*	*⅜″ diam. × 5″ long*
Uprights E	*6*	*Dowel*	*½″ diam. × 5½″ long*
Coupling Pin F	*1*	*Dowel*	*½″ diam. × 1⅛″ long*
Logs	*18*	*Dowel, Branches, etc.*	*15″ × ¾″ × ¾″*

You will also need: *two ⁷⁄₁₆″ screw eyes, eight 2″*
wheels and two axles.

INSTRUCTIONS

1. Cut all pieces to finished size and shape (see Illus. 33 and 34). The logs can be made from dowelling, old broom handles, branches, or square stock.
2. Drill the coupling pin hole in the bottom of the base (A) ½″ in diameter and ½″ deep—it should be 1″ from the front end and centered.
3. Drill the holes for the uprights (E) on the top side of the base (A). All centers are to be ½″ from the edge; the four uprights on the ends to be 1¼″ from the

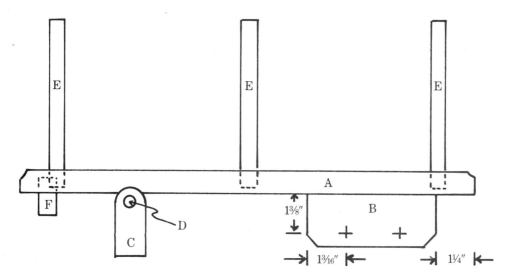

Illus. 33.   Logging Trailer, side view

ends; the two middle uprights centered. Drill ⅝" deep.

4. On the base (A) drill two holes 4" from the front edge and ½" from the sides to accept ⁷⁄₁₆" screw eyes.

5. The top edge can be routered with a ¼" cove bit for a more finished look.

6. In each stand piece (C) drill a hole with ⅜" diameter centered and down ⅜" from the top edge. The dowel (D) for the stand will be fitted into these holes.

7. In the wheel block (B) drill axle holes as per Illus. 34 to accept either screws or dowels. Also cut the bottom corners of the wheel block to 45°.

8. Glue the six uprights (E) in place.

9. Glue the wheel block (B) centered and in 1¼" from the rear end.

10. Screw the ⁷⁄₁₆" screw eyes in place under the base. Check that the dowel is a snug fit. Run the dowel (D) through the screw eyes and attach both stands (C); secure to dowel with glue and a small finishing nail. The dowel should turn snugly in the screw eyes.

11. Glue the coupling pin (F) into the coupling pin hole.

12. Sand the logs well.

13. Finish as desired, then mount two 2" wheels on each side of the axles.

14. Load the logs and you're ready to roll!

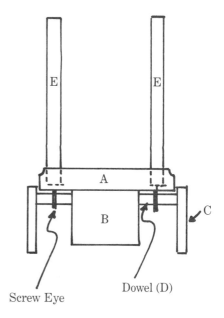

Illus. 34.   Logging Trailer, end view

Car Carrier

Illus. 35.   Loaded Car Carrier

Illus. 36.   Car Carrier with ramp down

CUTTING LIST

Coupling Pin A	1	Dowel	½" diam. × 1⅛" long
Wheel Block B	1	Pine	4½" × 2½" × 1⅞"
Stands C	2	Mahogany	2½" × 1" × ¼"
Upper Deck D	1	Pine	16⅝" × 4¼" × ¾"
Lower Deck E	1	Pine	16" × 4¼" × ¾"
Front Vertical Deck Supports F	2	Mahogany	5½" × 2½" × ⅜"
Rear Vertical Deck Supports G	2	Mahogany	5½" × 2½" × ⅜"
Ramp H	1	Pine	7" × 4¼" × ¾"
Ramp Latches I	2	Mahogany	1½" × ⅜" × ¼"
Rear Deck Support J	2	Dowel	¼" diam. × 5¹⁄₁₆" long
Stand Dowel K	1	Dowel	⅜" diam. × 5" long.

You will also need: *a piece of scrap wood 16" × 4¼" × ½" to make the depressions for the vehicle wheels to fit into. You will also need screws, hinges, eight 2" diameter wheels and axles. Car designs can be found in Simple Toys on Wheels. Keep the vehicles less than 5" long or they will not fit on the Car Carrier decks without bumping into one another.*

INSTRUCTIONS

1. Cut all parts to finished size and shape as per Illus. 37–41.
2. Cut the wheel depressions in the decks (E and D) as follows (see Illus. 41). Place the scrap wood between the upper and lower decks and clamp the pieces together. Using a 1¼" diameter bit drill the six holes to a depth of 1½". Unclamp and you'll have your wheel depressions.
3. Bevel the ends of the ramp (H) and the rear ends of the lower and upper deck (Illus. 37).
4. Drill the axle holes in the wheel block (B) as in Illus. 37. The hole size will depend on which method you use to mount the wheels. They can turn freely on large screws or they can be mounted on the ends of dowels which run through the wheel base.
5. Glue the wheel block to the underside of the bottom deck.
6. Drill the holes for the screw eyes on the underside of the bottom deck 3¾" from the front end and ½" from the edge.
7. Drill the hole for the coupling pin on the underside of the lower deck ½" in diameter and ½" deep. Glue the coupling pin (A) in place (Illus. 37).
8. Using screws, join the decks at the front end using the two front vertical deck supports (F) shown in Illus. 38. All vertical deck supports are cut the same. The two at the front are screwed in place. The top of the dowels which run

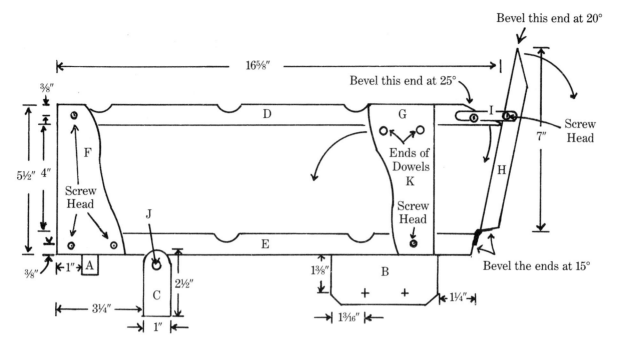

Bevel this end at 20°

Bevel this end at 25°

16⅝″

⅜″

D

G

Screw
Head

Ends of
Dowels
K

I

7″

Screw
Head

F

H

5½″ 4″

Screw
Head

J

Screw
Head

⅜″

1″ A

E

2½″

C

3¼″

1″

1⅜″

B

Bevel the ends at 15°

1¾₁₆″

1¼″

Illus. 37.   Car Carrier, side view

between the rear supports must be down ¾″ from the top edge. Place a washer between the screws and the decks.

9. Drill ¼″ holes for the dowels in the other two rear vertical deck supports (G) shown in Illus. 39 and join the supports with ¼″ dowels. Using screws, mount this set of supports near the loading end of the lower ramp. Place flat washers between the screws and upper deck. Put a screw in the upper deck to act as a "stop."

10. Put the screw eyes in place under the lower deck. Feed the ⅜″ dowel through the screw eyes. This should be a snug fit. Attach the stands (C) to each end of the dowel using glue and a set nail to secure them.

11. Now put the truck on its side with the decks parallel as in Illus. 37. Holding the ramp in place, position the ramp latches (I) as shown and screw one into each side. Now add a screw on each side of the upper ramp for the ramp latches to hook on.

12. Position your hinge or hinges at the bottom of the ramp and end of the lower deck, and mark and drill the screw sites for mounting the hinges.

13. Finish as desired.

14. Mount the ramp latches (I); hinge the ramp (H) in place and add the wheels. Put flat washers between each pair of wheels and between the wheels and the wheel base.

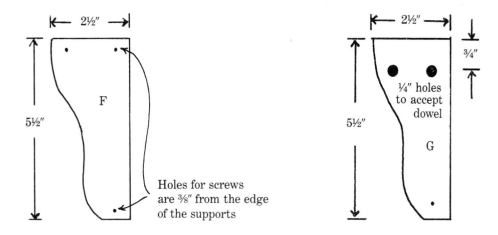

Illus. 38. Front vertical deck support

Holes for screws
are ⅜″ from the edge
of the supports

2½″

5½″

F

Illus. 39. Rear vertical deck support

2½″

¾″

¼″ holes
to accept
dowel

5½″

G

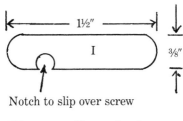

1½″

I

⅜″

Notch to slip over screw

Illus. 40. Ramp latch

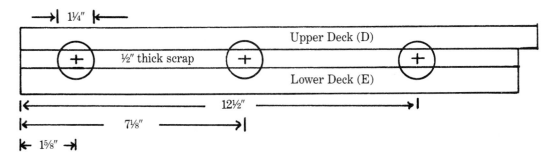

1¼″

Upper Deck (D)

½″ thick scrap

Lower Deck (E)

12½″

7⅛″

1⅝″

Illus. 41. Making wheel depressions for Car Carrier decks

SIMPLE TOYS ON WHEELS

The stock may be any thickness from ¾″ and up. I usually use 2″ stock. Laminated plywood gives a unique striped appearance and allows you to use scraps which would otherwise be discarded. A two-tone vehicle, such as one made from mahogany and pine, has more flash than a single-toned one. The wheels can be purchased from a toy supply company, cut on the band saw or drill press, or turned on the lathe.

GENERAL INSTRUCTIONS

1. Draw the pattern on grid paper or enlarge it on a copying machine, and transfer the design to your selected stock.
2. Cut the toy from the stock.
3. Sand all edges.
4. Drill axle holes about ⅜″ up from the bottom edge and in about 1″ from each end for use with 1¼″ diameter wheels. You will have to adjust these distances if you use wheels of different diameters. Also, the diameter of the axle holes will depend on wheel size and the type of axle you use.

Method A: each wheel can be attached using a large screw on which the wheel may turn freely. Put a flat washer between the wheel and body.

Method B: The wheels can be mounted on the ends of a dowel which runs through the body of the toy. If you use ¼″ dowel, make the axle hole ⁵⁄₁₆″ in diameter to allow the dowel to turn freely. Put a flat washer between the wheel and toy body.

5. Edges may be finished by sanding off the sharp corners or by running the toy past a ¼″ or ⅛″ cove bit or corner rounding bit on a stationary router.
6. Drill the "windows."

Method A: Using a spur bit, drill to a very shallow depth which will simply score the surface of the wood. A ¾″ diameter bit is a good size.

Method B: Drill a hole all the way through the toy.

7. Sand the sides.
8. Mount the wheels.
9. Finish as desired.

Sedan I

Each square = 1″

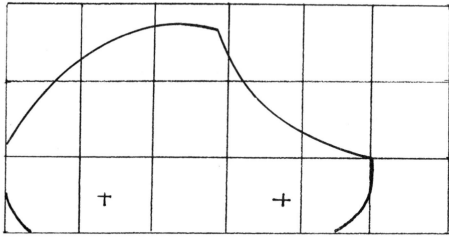

Illus. 42.

Sedan II

Each square = 1″

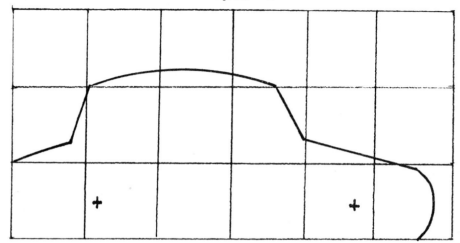

Illus. 43.

Sedan III

Each square = 1″

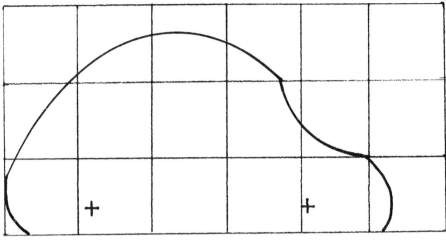

Illus. 44.

Racer

Each square = 1″

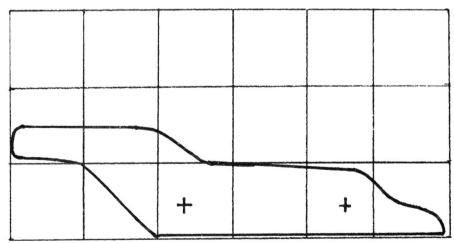

Illus. 45.

Van I

Each square = 1″

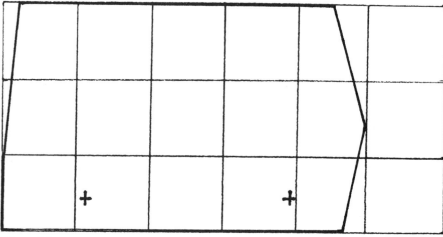

Illus. 46.

Van II

Each square = 1″

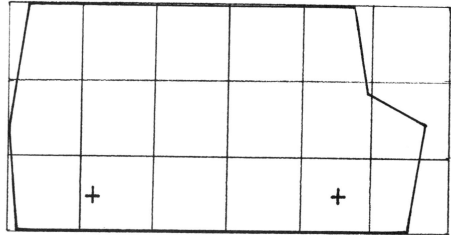

Illus. 47.

Station Wagon

Each square = 1″

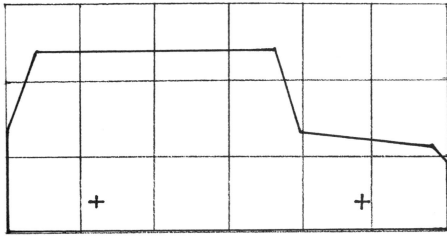

Illus. 48.

The Spoiler

Each square = 1″

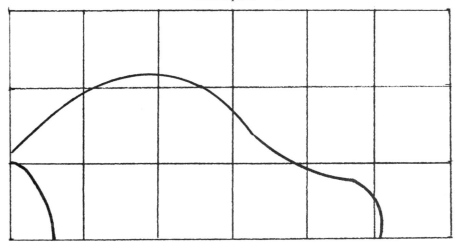

Illus. 49.

Bug

Each square = 1"

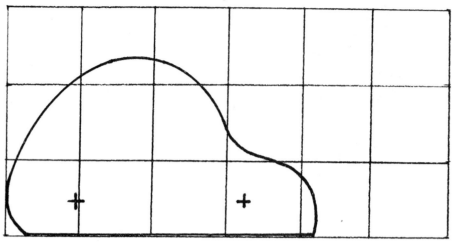

Illus. 50.

Half Ton

Each square = 1"

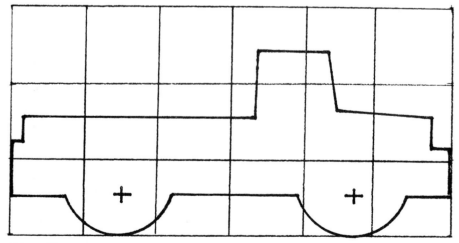

Illus. 51.

Lace-Up Roller Skate

After you cut and sand the skate, drill holes to accept about 6 screw eyes down each side of the front surface to act as eyelets for the shoelace. Finish the roller skate as desired then mount the wheels and put the screw eyes in place. Add a shoelace about 45″ in length and that completes the toy!

Illus. 52.

Each square = 1″

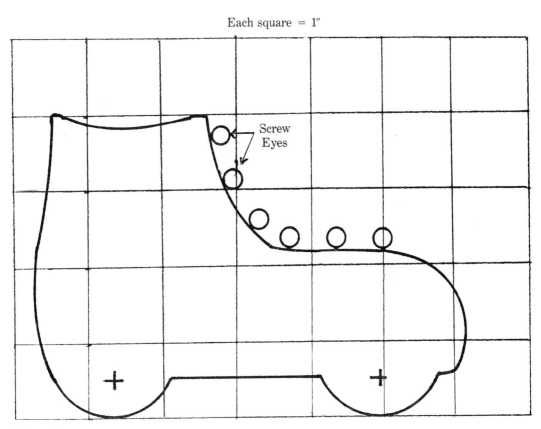

Screw Eyes

Illus. 53.

Elephant

I glue ⅜″ "wiggle" eyes (plastic bubbles with free-rolling metal beads inside) on to the animals. Or, you can paint the eyes on. Add ears, whiskers and tail as necessary. Leather is a good material to cut these from, as it's durable and will not fray. Attach the ears and tail with a short nail which has a large head (not a finishing nail).

Illus. 54.

Each square = 1″

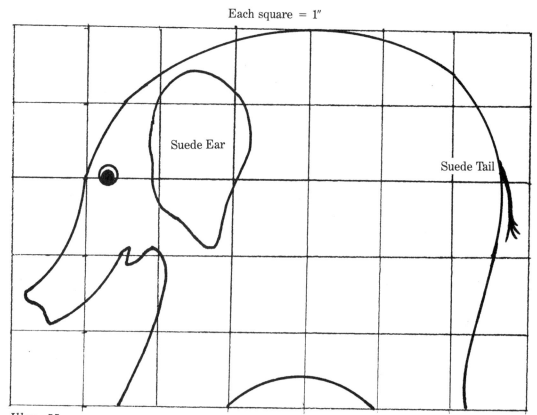

Suede Ear

Suede Tail

Illus. 55.

Horse

Illus. 56.

Each square = 1″

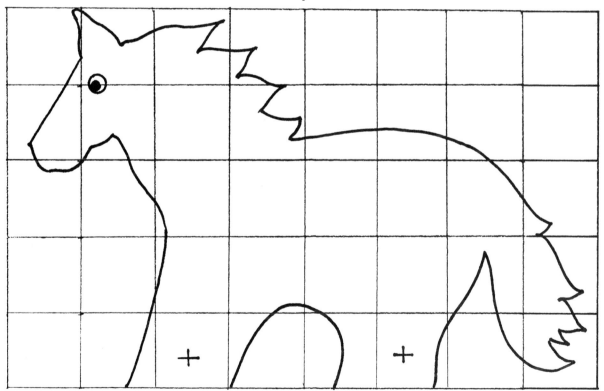

Illus. 57.

Rabbit

Illus. 58.

Each square = 1″

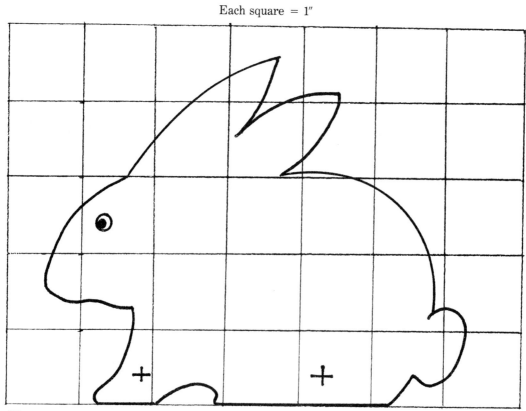

Illus. 59.

Plane

Illus. 60.

After cutting out the pattern and finishing
the edges, attach the wings using glue and
screws. Countersink the screws and cover
the heads with a wood filler or with plugs.
Attach the tailpiece in the same manner.
Cut out the propeller and drill a hole
through the center large enough to allow it
to turn freely on the screw you mount it
with. Mount the propeller, putting a flat
washer between it and the nose of the plane.

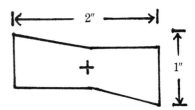

Illus. 61. Plane propeller

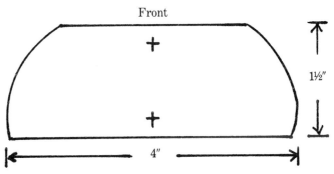

Illus. 62. Plane tailpiece

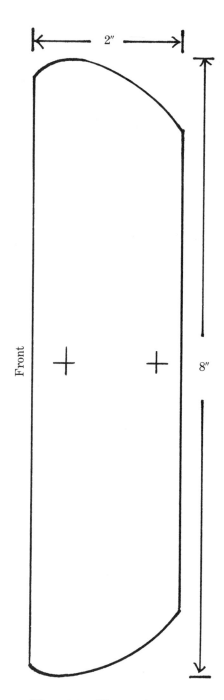

2″

Front

8″

Illus. 63.   Plane wing

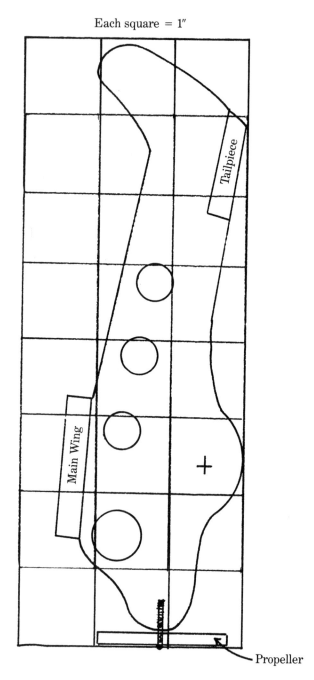

Each square = 1″

Tailpiece

Main Wing

Propeller

Illus. 64.   Plane body

48

Five-Car Train

Illus. 65.

A combination of contrasting woods gives this train a more interesting appearance. The coupling mechanism for this train involves small metal parts (screw hooks and screw eyes) which could be unscrewed—therefore this train isn't recommended for young children who might put these in their mouths.

INSTRUCTIONS

1. Cut all engine pieces to their finished size and shape (Illus. 66, 67 and 68).
2. Add "windows" by just scoring the wood with a spur bit **OR** by drilling all the way through the piece.
3. Attach parts A and B to the base (Illus. 66).
4. Drill the hole in part A to accommodate the smokestack, then glue the stack in place. The middle of the smokestack may be drilled out to a depth of 1″ or so if desired. Use a ½″ bit.
5. Sand off all sharp edges and sand all surfaces.
6. Cut all pieces of the hopper to their finished size and shape (Illus. 69, 70 and 71).
7. Attach the sides and ends using glue and finishing nails. Do not put nails in where you will be drilling the axle holes.
8. Round off the corners and sand off all sharp edges.
9. Cut all pieces of the log carrier to their finished size and shape (Illus. 72 and 73).
10. Drill the holes in the base, then glue the dowels in place.
11. Sand off all sharp edges.
12. Cut the box car to finished size (Illus. 74 and 75).
13. Cut all pieces of the caboose to finished size (Illus. 76, 77 and 78).
14. Add "windows" on two sides of piece A and on all four sides of piece C (Illus. 76).
15. Glue parts A, B, C and D together. An elastic makes a good substitute clamp.
16. For assembly, drill holes in the rear end of the engine, the front of the caboose

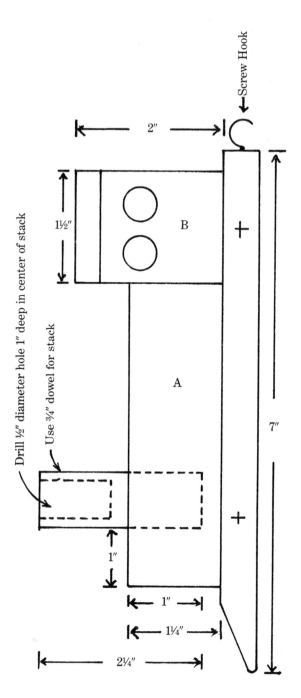

Screw Hook

2″

1½″

B

Drill ½″ diameter hole 1″ deep in center of stack

Use ¾″ dowel for stack

A

7″

1″

1″

1¼″

2¼″

Illus. 66.   Train engine, side view

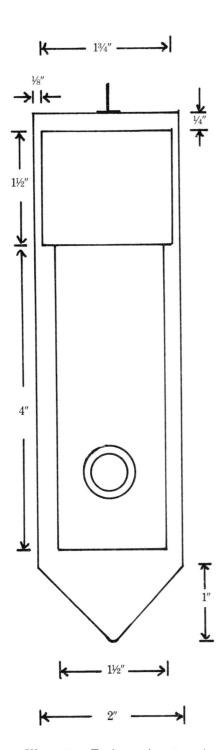

Illus. 67.   Train engine, top view

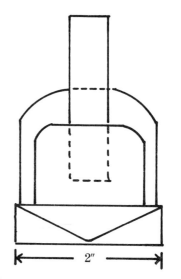

Illus. 68.   Train engine, front view

51

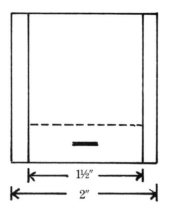

Illus. 69.   Hopper, front view

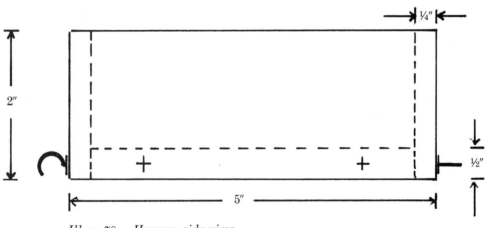

Illus. 70.   Hopper, side view

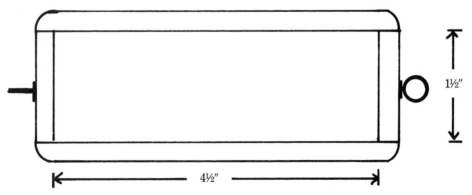

Illus. 71.   Hopper, top view

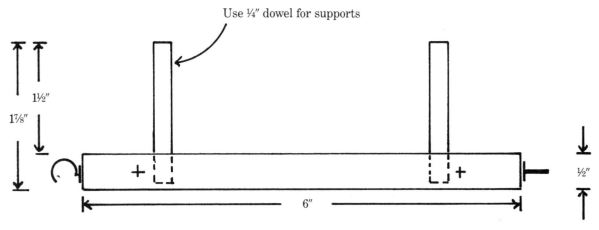

Use ¼″ dowel for supports

1½″

1⅞″

6″

½″

Illus. 72.   Log Carrier, side view

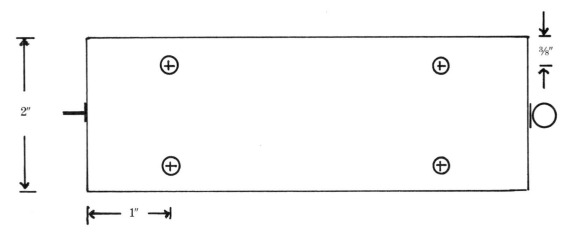

⅜″

2″

1″

Illus. 73.   Log Carrier, top view

and each end of the middle cars to accommodate the screw eyes and hooks which serve as the train's coupling mechanism.

17. Drill the axle holes in the bases. The size of these will be determined by the size of the holes in the wheels you use and whether you mount the wheels using dowels or screws.

18. Finish the train as desired and attach wheels. I used 1″ diameter wheels for the cars and front engine, and 1¼″ diameter wheels for the rear engine.

19. Screw in the screw eyes and hooks to connect the cars, placing a flat washer between each and the cars.

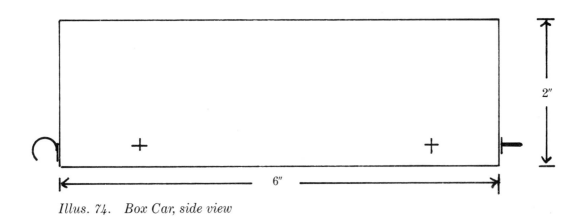

Illus. 74.   Box Car, side view

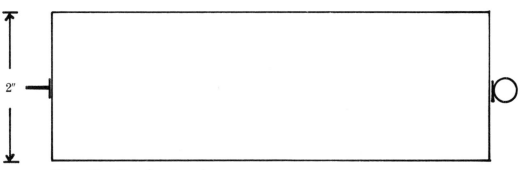

Illus. 75.   Box Car, top view

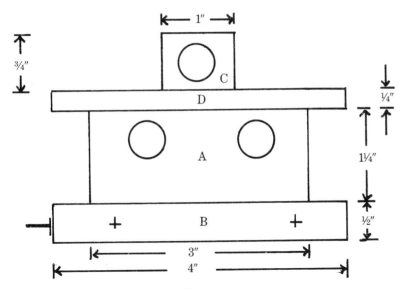

Illus. 76.   Caboose, side view

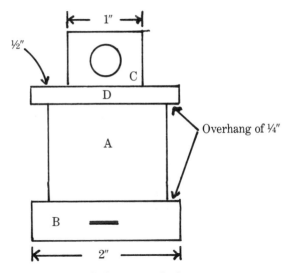

Illus. 77.   Caboose, end view

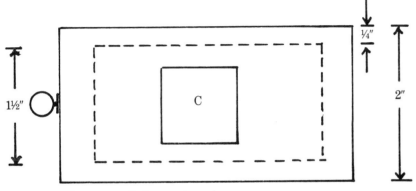

Illus. 78.   Caboose, top view

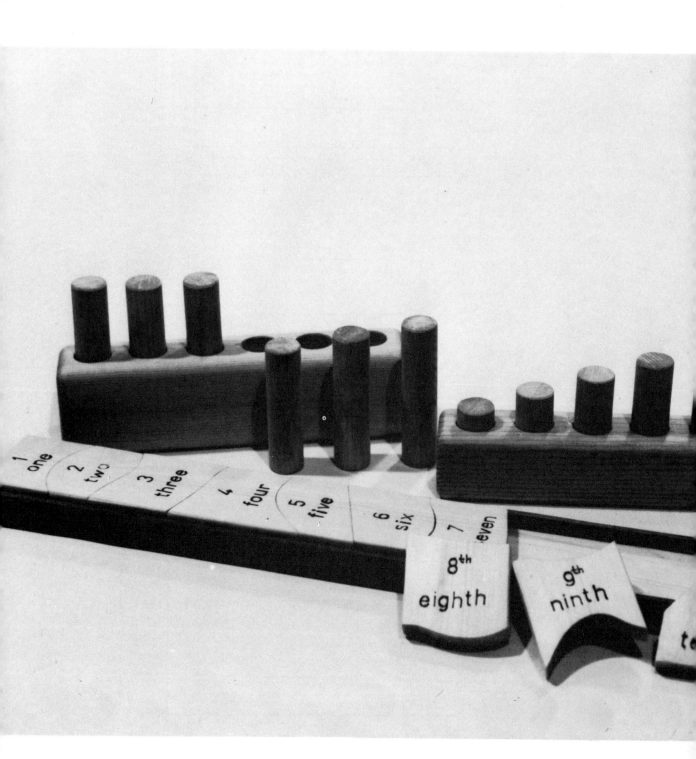

PUZZLES

Reversible Counting Puzzle

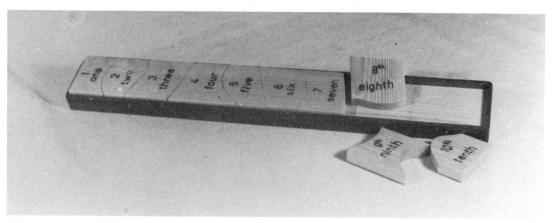

Illus. 79.

In addition to reinforcing counting from one to ten, this puzzle also helps develop hand/eye coordination. Using both sides of the puzzle adds variety and challenge.

CUTTING LIST

Ends	2	*3¼" × 1" × ¼"*
Sides	2	*20¾" × 1" × ¼"*
Base	1	*20" × 2⁹⁄₁₆" × ½"*
Top	1	*20" × 2½ × ¾"*

INSTRUCTIONS

1. Cut all pieces to size as per Illus. 80, 81 and 82.

2. Cutting the puzzle pieces will result in reduction of their combined length due to your saw cuts. Sand these pieces on all edges, then check their fit on the base board. They should fit loosely with about ¹⁄₁₆" of play around the edges. Adjust the length of the base board to fit the puzzle pieces. Sand the base smooth on the inside face as it's easiest to reach at this time.

3. Trim the sides to exact length, then attach the sides using glue and finishing nails. Attach the ends (they will over-hang slightly), then trim them to an exact fit. Round off all corners and sand smooth any sharp edges.

4. Finish as desired.

5. Number and letter the pieces. A small plastic stencil will help give a neat appearance. A soft-tip pen can be used or you can paint the letters and numbers on. Options for the other side include one through ten spelled out in a foreign language, color gradations shown by painting the squares the colors of the spectrum, or the ordinal forms of the numbers as shown by the 3 pieces at right in Illus. 79.

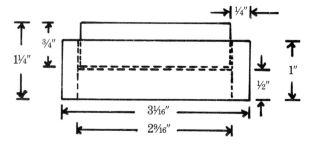

Illus. 80.   Counting Puzzle, end view

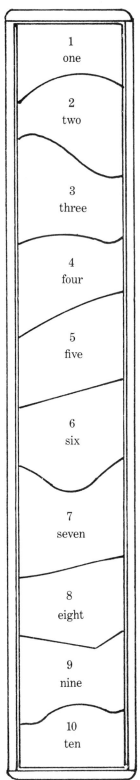

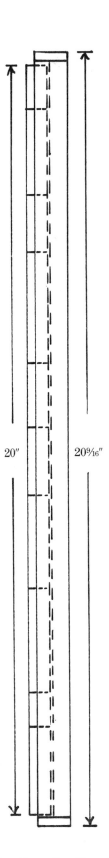

1
one

2
two

3
three

4
four

5
five

6
six

7
seven

8
eight

9
nine

10
ten

20"   20⁹⁄₁₆"

Illus. 81.   Counting Puzzle

Illus. 82.   Counting Puzzle, side view

Size Discrimination Puzzles

Illus. 83.

CUTTING LIST
Puzzle I

Base	1	9½″ × 2″ × 2″	
Pegs	6	9½″ × 2″ × 2″ 1″ diam. dowel: 2¼″, 2″, 1¾″, 1½″, and 1″ in length	

Puzzle II

Base	1	9½″ × 2″ × 1½″	
Pegs	6	9½″ × 2″ × 1½″ 1″ diam. dowel: 4″, 3½″, 3″, 2½″, 2″ and 1½″ in length	

INSTRUCTIONS

1. Cut the base and dowels to the finished size (Illus. 84, 85 and 86).
2. Drill 1¹⁄₁₆″ diameter holes to the correct depths as per Illus. 84 or 85, depending on the puzzle you are making. The hole layout is shown in Illus. 86.
3. Round all edges of the base using a ¼″ corner rounding bit on the router or sand the edges well.
4. Sand all pieces.
5. Finish as desired.

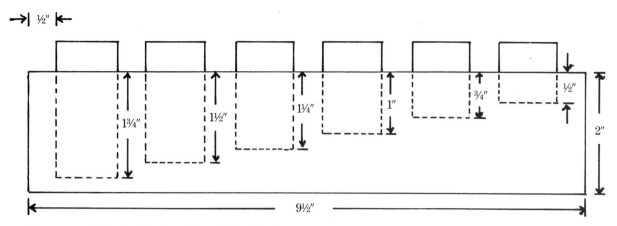

Illus. 84. Discrimination Puzzle I, side view

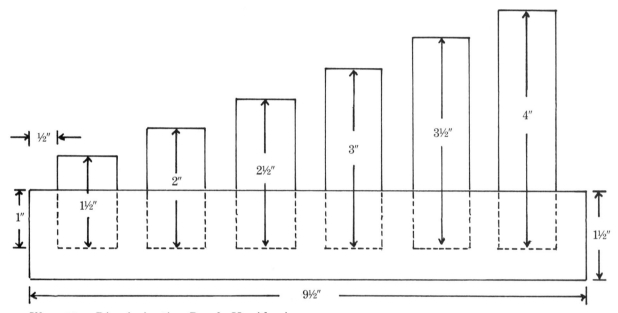

Illus. 85. Discrimination Puzzle II, side view

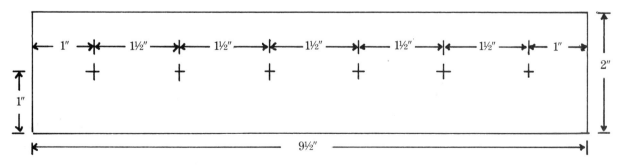

Illus. 86. Hole layout (top view) for both

Tray Puzzles

Illus. 87.

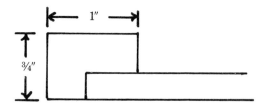

Illus. 88. Edge detail

The picture on a puzzle may be a decal, a piece of wallpaper, or may be painted on. Tray Puzzles can be constructed from hardboard, plywood or solid wood. The diagrams show ¼″ hardboard in use for the puzzle pieces and backing.

INSTRUCTIONS

1. Apply the picture to the wood and cut it out in an interesting puzzle pattern.
2. To make a puzzle tray simply glue strips around the edge of the piece of wood to be used as the backing. Measure your finished picture to determine the tray size needed. Add 1½″ to the width and the length. Cut out the back.
3. Glue ¾″ wide strips around the upper edges of your backing.
4. Finish as desired. If you want a more "finished" edge, use thicker edges, rabbet them and mitre the corners (Illus. 88).

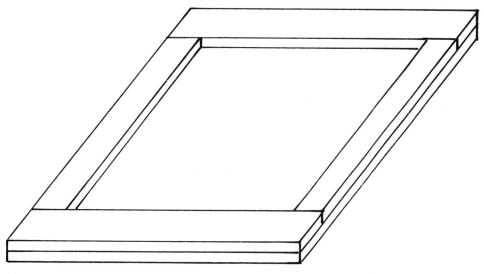

Illus. 89.   Puzzle backing

A1. Apple Bank

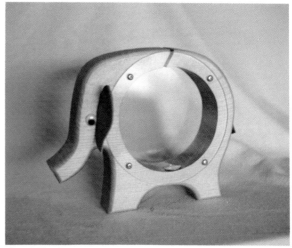

A2. Elephant Bank

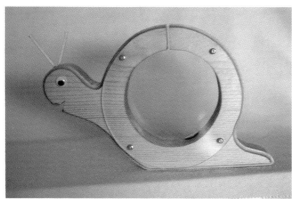

A3. Snail Bank

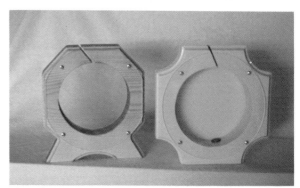

A4. Octagon I Bank (left) and Octagon II Bank (right)

A5. Rabbit Bank

A6. Owl Bank

B1. *An assortment of Simple Toys on Wheels.*

B2. *Truck Fleet, clockwise from bottom right: Car Carrier with Cab I; Stock Trailer; Transport Trailer; and Logging Trailer with Cab II.*

B

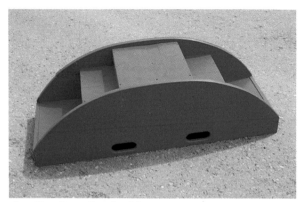

C1. The Step Set doubles as . . .

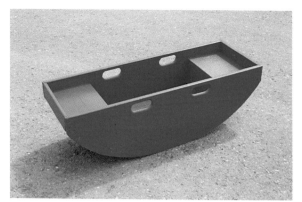

C2. . . . a Teeter Totter when flipped over.

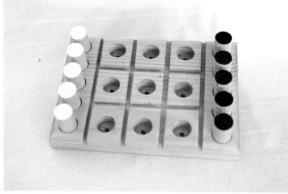

C3. Tic Tac Toe

C4. Puzzles: upper left, Size Discrimination Puzzles; center, Tray Puzzles; and bottom, Reversible Counting Puzzle.

C5. Balance Beams and Blocks

D. Indoor Play Center featuring a puppet theatre/closet, desk, toy boxes/seats, and upper platform with rails.

D

WOOD AND PLEXIGLAS BANKS

It's always nice to see your savings grow, and the Plexiglas sides on these banks make that possible. The removal of three screws is all that is necessary to remove the money. Using Robertson head screws gives improved durability. If the screw holes in the wood wear out, simply install the Plexiglas with the next larger screw size.

I use 2" stock for the banks. If you cut out the center carefully, the scrap circle of wood can be used to make Simple Toys on Wheels, or blocks for the Building Blocks set.

GENERAL INSTRUCTIONS

1. Draw the pattern chosen on grid paper or enlarge it on a copying machine, and transfer the design to your stock.
2. Cut around the outside edge.
3. Cut the money slot, and then cut out the inner circle.
4. Sand all edges smooth.
5. Rout the outer edges with a ¼" corner rounding bit for an edge like the one on the Elephant or Rabbit Bank (Illus. 97 and 109). Use a cove bit for an edge like the Piggy Bank, Snail or Octagon II (Illus. 95, 99 and 115).
6. Keeping the protective paper on, cut two Plexiglas circles, making them as large as possible to fit the bank you're making. The size will depend on which pattern you chose. Sand the edges.
7. Drill your ³⁄₁₆" diameter holes for the screws in each piece of Plexiglas. Set the holes equidistant around the circle's edge and in about ⅜" from the edge. Drill with a fairly light pressure and ease up when you near the far side, as the Plexiglas will tend to crack under heavy drilling pressure.
8. Place the Plexiglas on the bank and mark the centers of the screw holes. Repeat this on the other side.
9. Drill the screw holes in the wood to accommodate #6 × ¾" roundhead screws (four on each side).
10. Sand all faces and any rough areas or sharp edges.

11. Finish the wooden part of the bank with oil, varnish, paint or a combination.

12. Peel off the protective paper from the inner side of the Plexiglas and using #6 × ¾″ Robertson head screws, attach both pieces to the wood. Leave the outer paper on until all work has been completed to avoid scratching the Plexiglas.

13. For animal ears and tails transfer the pattern required to suede or another suitable material. After cutting them out, attach them using ½″ nails with a large head. Glue on "wiggle" eyes—an elastic makes a good clamp for holding these in place.

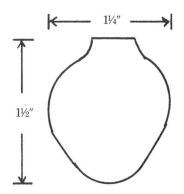

Illus. 90.   Piggy ear

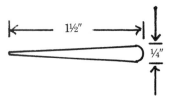

Illus. 91.   Tail for Piggy and Hippopotamus

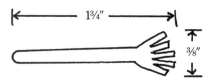

Illus. 92.   Elephant tail

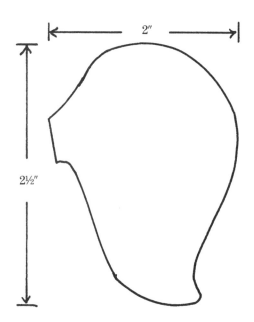

Illus. 93.   Elephant ear

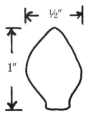

Illus. 94.   Hippopotamus ear

Piggy Bank

Illus. 95.

Each square = 2″

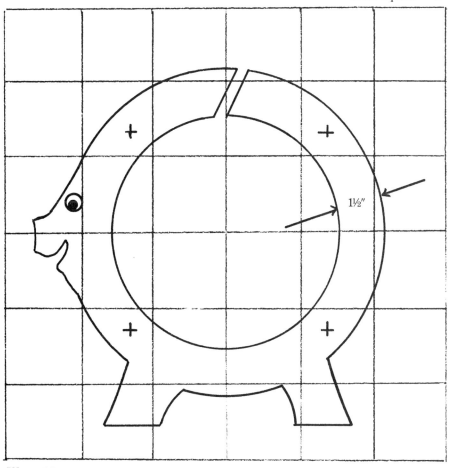

1½″

Illus. 96.

Elephant Bank

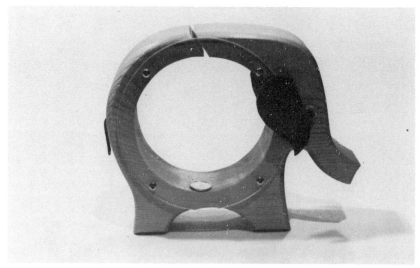

Illus. 97.

Each square = 2″

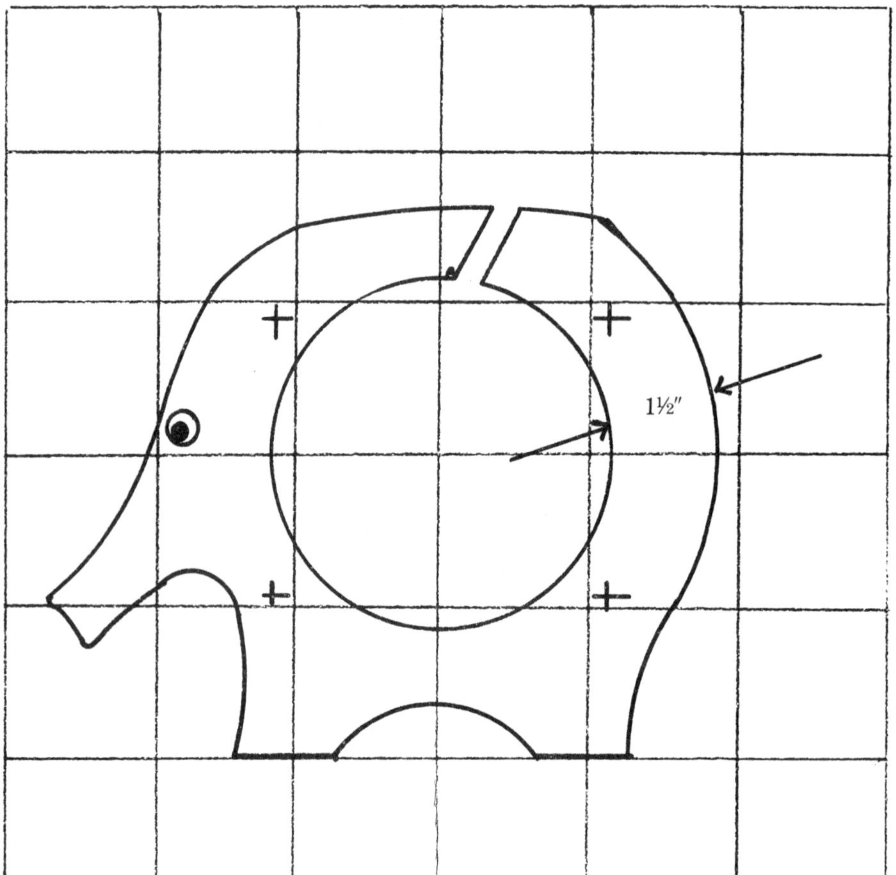

1½″

Illus. 98.

Snail Bank

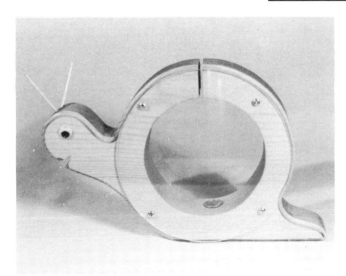

Illus. 99.

The snail's antennae are 2½″ finishing nails painted yellow or brown. Drill snug pilot holes for these at different angles.

Each square = 2″

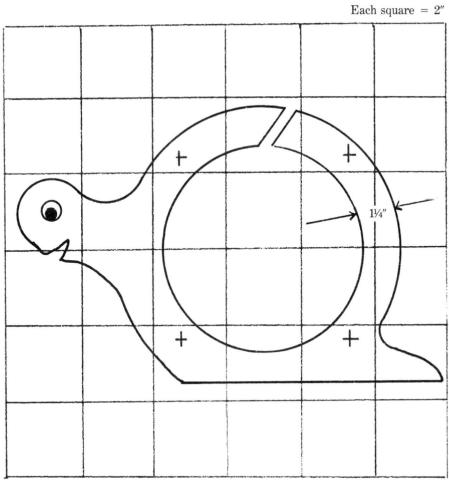

Illus. 100.

Duck Bank

Each square = 2″

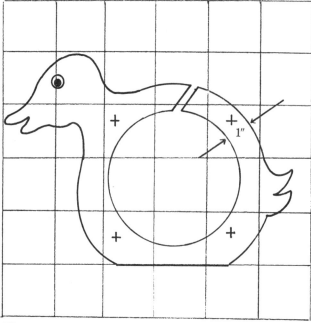

Illus. 101.

Hippopotamus Bank

Each square = 2″

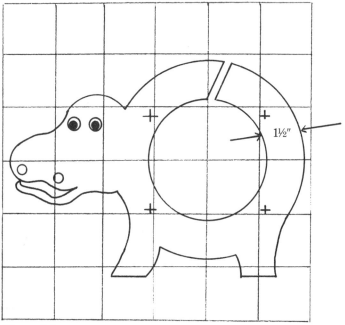

Illus. 102.

Owl Bank

Illus. 103.

Each square = 2″

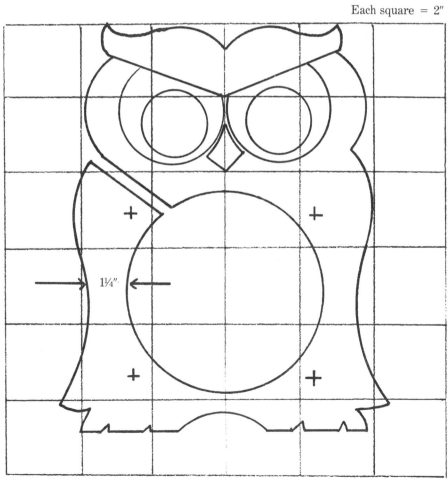

1¼″

Illus. 104.

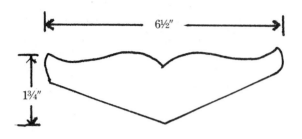

Illus. 105.   Top of Owl's head

The owl can have eyes, beak and forehead painted on, or they can be made of wood as per Illus. 105, 106 and 107. If you make them from wood, glue the forehead piece on first, then add the eyes and finally glue the beak in place.

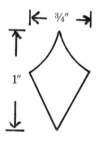

Illus. 106.   Owl's beak

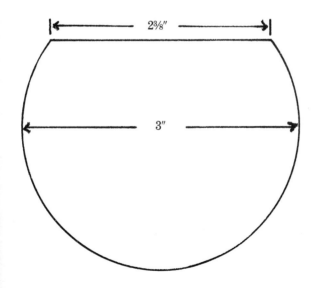

Illus. 107.   Owl eye

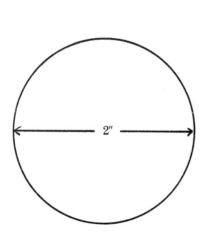

Illus. 108.   Inner Owl eye

Rabbit Bank

Illus. 109.

Each square = 2″

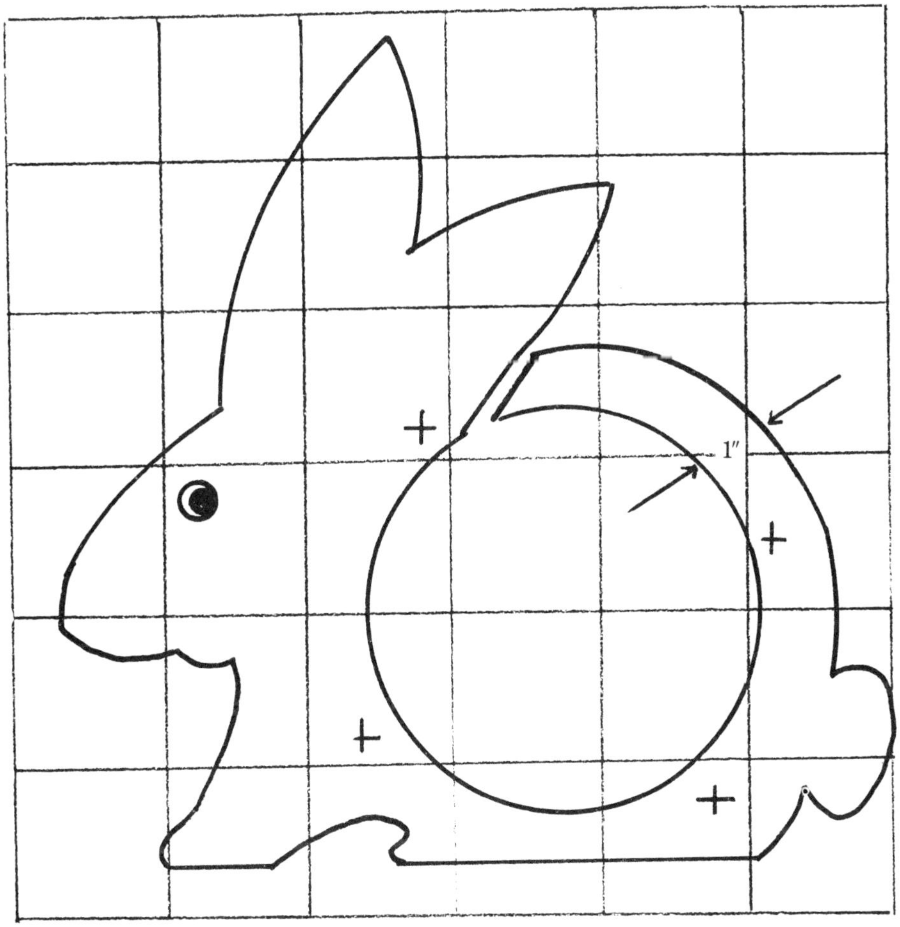

Illus. 110.

Apple Bank

You may want to use different colors of Plexiglas such as red Plexiglas for the apple. If the rear piece of Plexiglas is red and the front one is clear you will have color and still be able to see your money easily.

Each square = 2″

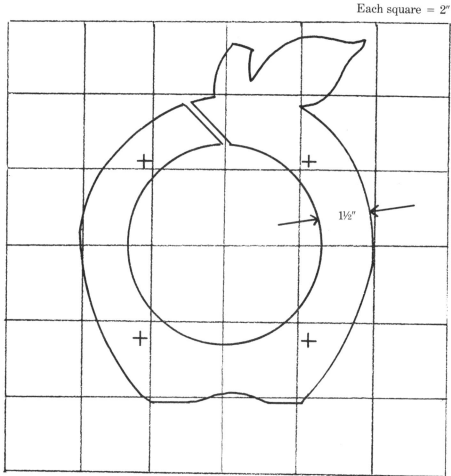

1½″

Square Bank

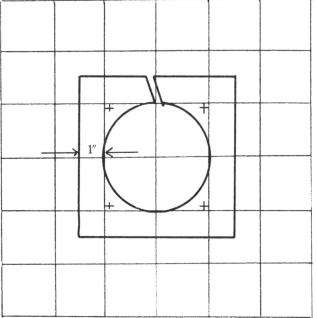

Each square = 2"

1"

Illus. 113.
The Plexiglas
may be cut in
either a square or
a circular shape

Octagon I Bank

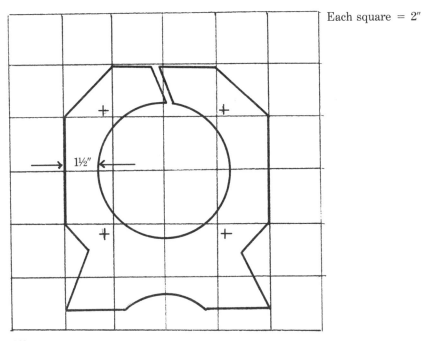

Each square = 2"

1½"

Illus. 114.

Circle Bank

Illus. 115.

Each square = 2″

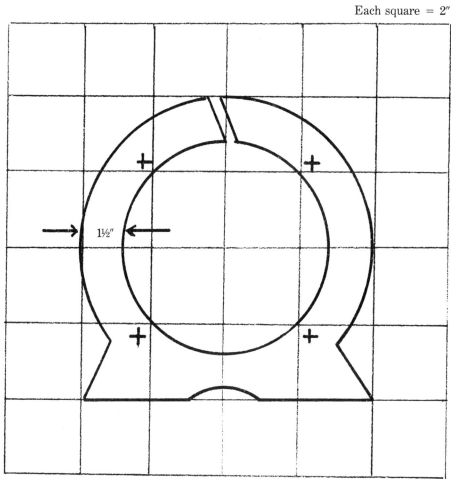

1½″

Illus. 116.

76

Octagon II Bank

Illus. 117.

Each square = 2"

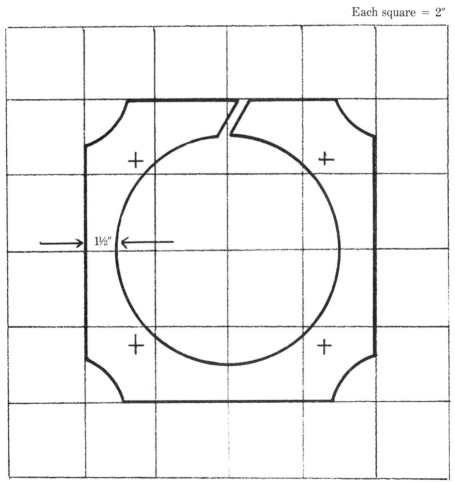

1½"

Illus. 118.

YARD TOYS

Balance Beams and Blocks

These Balance Beams have a great deal of versatility and play value because they can be arranged in a variety of patterns. They help develop imagination as well as balance and coordination. The bases can be made from 4″ stock, or you can laminate three 2″ × 4″s to give you 3½″ stock.

CUTTING LIST

Bases	5		3½″ × 3½″
Dowel Pegs	10	Dowel	¾″ diam. × 2¾″ long
Beams	4	Plywood	48″ × 4″ × ¾″

INSTRUCTIONS

1. Cut all bases to finished size (Illus. 119). Make five bases or more.

2. Drill the holes for the dowels ¾″ in diameter and 2″ deep.
3. Round all edges using a ¼″ corner rounding bit.
4. Glue the dowels in place.
5. Finish with an exterior paint.
6. Cut all beams from ¾″ plywood and round the corners (Illus. 120). Cut four or more beams.
7. Drill the holes ¹³⁄₁₆″ in diameter for the dowels to fit into.
8. Round off the edges using a ¼″ corner rounding bit.
9. Finish with an exterior paint.

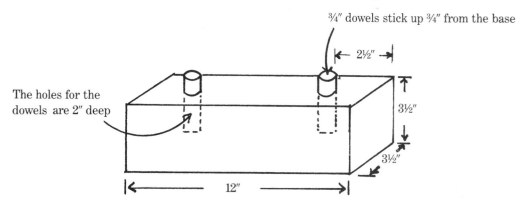

¾″ dowels stick up ¾″ from the base

← 2½″ →

The holes for the dowels are 2″ deep

3½″

3½″

12″

Illus. 119.   Base for Balance Beam

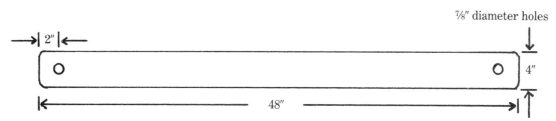

⅞″ diameter holes

2″

4″

48″

Illus. 120.   Balance Beam diagram

Stilts

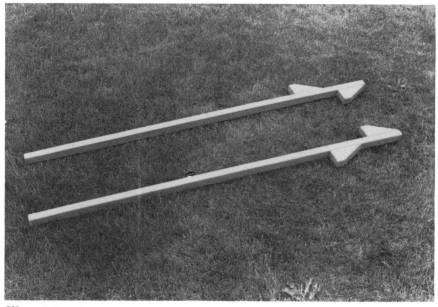

Illus. 121.

CUTTING LIST

Uprights	*2*	*72″ × 2″ × 2″*
Foot Rests	*4*	*72″ × 3″ × 1½″*

INSTRUCTIONS

1. Cut 2″ × 2″s to 72″ (6′) lengths. Planing these to 1¼″ × 1¼″ size will make them lighter and easier to handle.
2. Cut 4 foot rests as per Illus. 122.
3. Round off all edges with a ¼″ corner rounding bit on the router.
4. Using glue and screws attach the foot rests to the 2″ × 2″s as per Illus. 123. Raise the height of the foot rests for older or more experienced children.
5. Finish with an exterior paint.

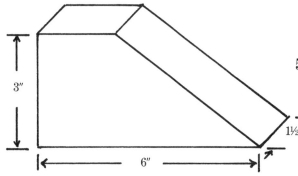

Illus. 122.   Foot rests for Stilts

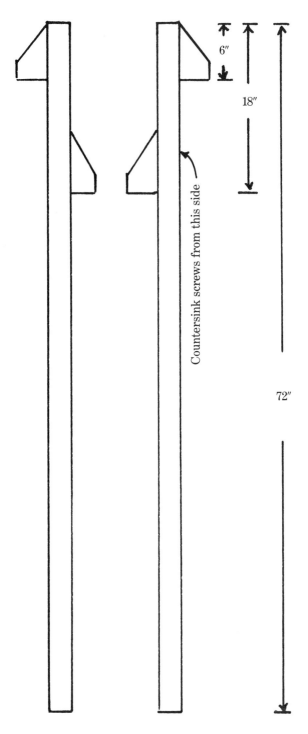

6″

18″

Countersink screws from this side

72″

Illus. 123.   Stilts diagram

83

Sandbox

Illus. 124.

Our sandbox provides hours of creative fun for our children and their friends. Many adventures are enacted there and the number of cities, space stations and roads made each year is amazing.

Sandboxes can be made with or without a bottom and lid. Having a bottom helps keep dirt from getting mixed with the sand. Having a lid keeps the rain out and, perhaps more importantly, keeps the neighborhood cats out. If you decide to put on a lid, place the sandbox against a fence, wall or tree so you can fasten the lid in the upright position to prevent its falling on the children.

The diagrams show a 4' × 8' sandbox with lid and corner seats.

CUTTING LIST

Sides	2	*95" × 10" × 2"*
Ends	2	*44" × 10" × 2"*
Bottom	1	*95" × 47" × ¼"*
Corner Seats	2	*12" × 12" × 2"; cut these in half on the diagonal to make 4 corner seats*
Side Reinforcement Pieces for Lid	2	*96" × 2" × 2"*
End and Middle Reinforcement Pieces for Lid	3	*45" × 2" × 2"*
Lid Top	1	*96" × 48" × ¼"*

You will also need: *screws and/or lag bolts, hinges and hardware to fasten the lid to a fence or wall when it is in the upright position.*

INSTRUCTIONS

1. Cut all pieces to their finished size and shape (Illus. 125, 126 and 127). Use at least ¼″ material for the bottom.
2. Assemble the four sides of the box using 3½″ long screws or lag bolts.
3. Screw or nail on the bottom piece.
4. Attach the corner seats with 3½″ long screws or lag bolts. For extra support attach strips of wood under each side.
5. Sand smooth and round off all edges.
6. Finish with exterior paint.
7. Cut lid to its finished size (Illus. 126). It has an overhang to serve as a handhold and to help keep the rain from seeping in.
8. Cut the 2″ × 2″ reinforcement pieces to their finished lengths.
9. Attach the lid to the reinforcement pieces using screws from the top side.
10. Hinge the lid to the back edge of the sandbox.
11. Finish with exterior paint.
12. Attach fasteners so the lid can be secured in an upright position.

SAND

Sand can be purchased at a sand and gravel pit or try using the yellow pages of your phone book under "sand." Buy washed sand as it is much cleaner to play in. Sand is sold by the cubic yard rather than by weight. While you will need about two thirds of a yard of sand to *fill* the box, one half yard will give lots of sand to play in.

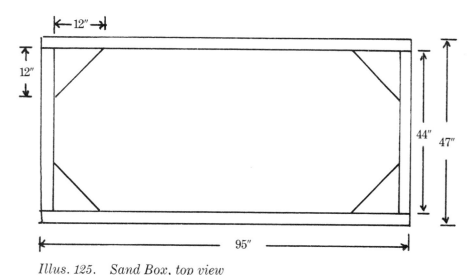

Illus. 125. Sand Box, top view

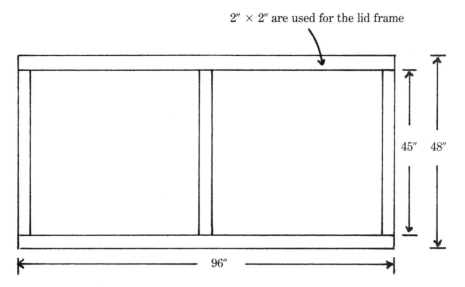

2″ × 2″ are used for the lid frame

45″   48″

96″

Illus. 126.   Sand Box lid viewed from the bottom

Lid hinged
at back

1″ overhang

Corner Seat
Support Strip

Illus. 127.   Sand Box, end view

Teeter-Totter/Step Set

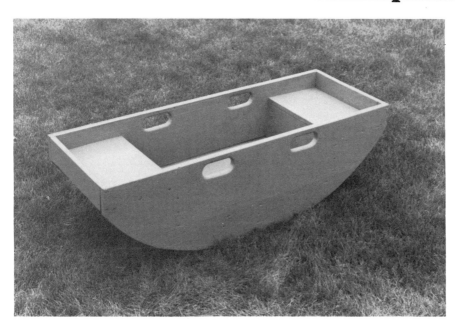

Illus. 128.

This is designed for younger children (two energetic youngsters of over fifty pounds might flip the Teeter-Totter over). When turned upside down, the Teeter-Totter becomes a Step Set.

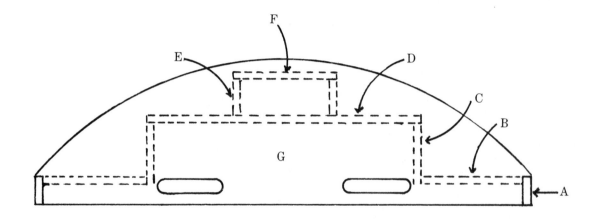

Illus. 129.

CUTTING LIST

End Piece A	2	16″ × 2½″ × ¾″
Lowest Step B	2	16″ × 10″ × ¾″
Middle Step		
Side C	2	16″ × 6″ × ¾″
Middle Step D	1	28″ × 16″ × ¾″
Top Step Side E	2	16″ × 3″ × ¾″
Top Step F	1	16″ × 12″ × ¾″
Sides G	2	48″ × 14″ × ¾″

INSTRUCTIONS

1. Cut all pieces to their finished size and shape (refer to Illus. 129 and 130).
2. Cut the handholds and sand their edges smooth. Or, instead of cutting handholds you can attach two pieces of 1½″ dowel across the Teeter-Totter for the children to hang on to.
3. Place the side pieces (G) vertically with their flat edge on your workbench.
4. Using glue and screws join the sides (G) with piece A at each end, then add B, C, D, E and F.
5. Round off all sharp edges and sand smooth.
6. Finish with exterior paint.

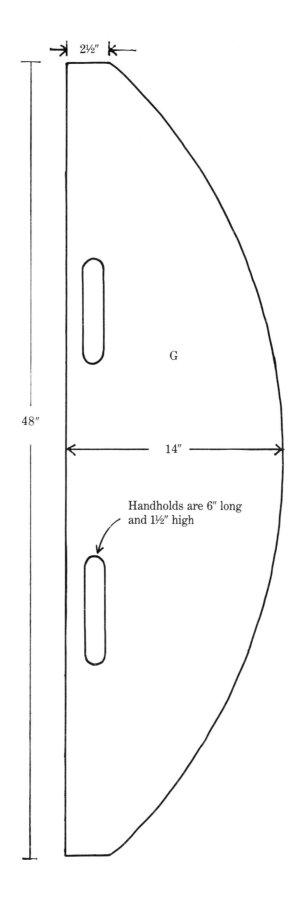

2½″

48″

G

14″

Handholds are 6″ long
and 1½″ high

Illus. 130.

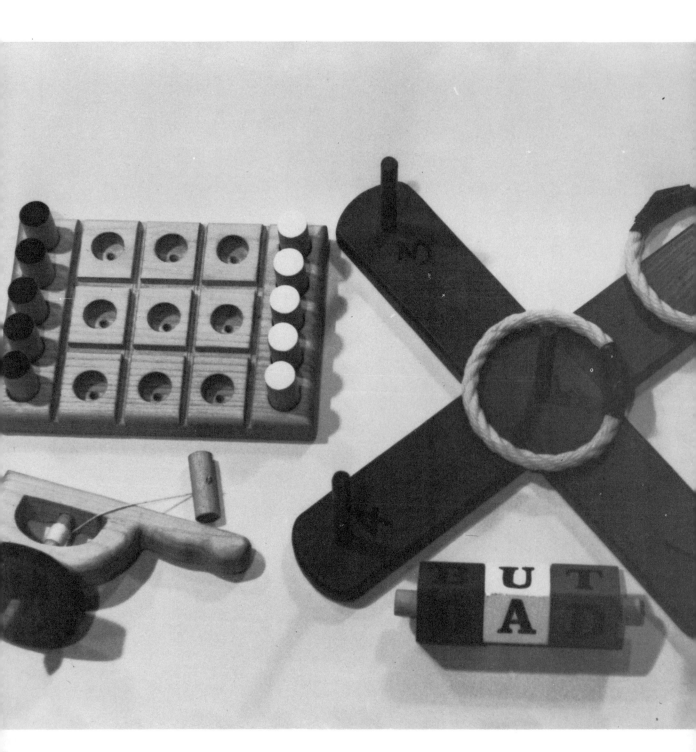

90

EASY-TO-MAKE/EASY-TO-PLAY

Ring Toss

Illus. 131.

CUTTING LIST

Base Board	*2*	*18″ × 3″ × ¾″*
Dowel	*5*	*⅝″ diam. × 4″ long*
Rings	*4*	

INSTRUCTIONS

1. Cut out the base boards and round the corners (Illus. 132).
2. Join the boards using a cross-lap joint.
3. Drill the holes for the dowels ⅝″ deep.
4. Round edges by sanding well or using a ¼″ corner rounding bit and a router.
5. Glue the dowels in place and sand the exposed ends smooth.
6. Sand and finish as desired. Numbers may be painted on the base by each dowel for a scoring system.
7. The rings should be about 5″ in diameter. Make 4 so each player can have two, using one of the following methods. They can be cut from ½″ plywood. Or, form a loop using rope, overlapping the ends and wrapping them tightly together with string and/or tape, or splice the ends together. They can also be made from tubing. Bamboo or plastic rings can often be found in variety or hobby shops.

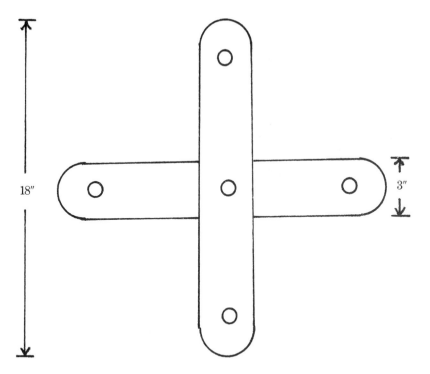

18″

3″

Illus. 132.   Ring Toss diagram

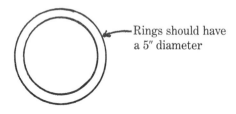

Rings should have
a 5″ diameter

Illus. 133.   Ring

93

Ball Through the Hole

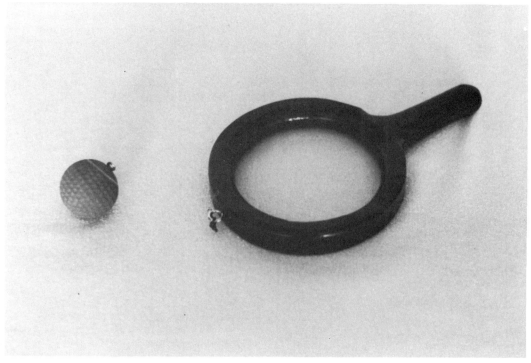

Illus. 134.

You will need: *a 8½″ × 5½″ piece of plywood for the paddle, and an 18″ length of string, a screw and a rubber ball.*

INSTRUCTIONS

1. From ½″ or ¾″ plywood cut out the paddle as per Illus. 135.
2. Cut out the inner area.
3. Finish all sharp edges by sanding well or using a corner rounding bit on the router.
4. Finish as desired.
5. Attach the string to the paddle using a screw eye, or simply tie the string around a screw which is then screwed into the wood.
6. The string should be about 18″ long and should be threaded through a heavy-weight needle, which is then pushed through a rubber ball and tied off on one end. You may find just the right size of ball in a pet store.
7. To play: hold the paddle in either hand and swing the ball in an arc above the paddle. Then move the paddle quickly under the ball and try to have it fall down through the hole.

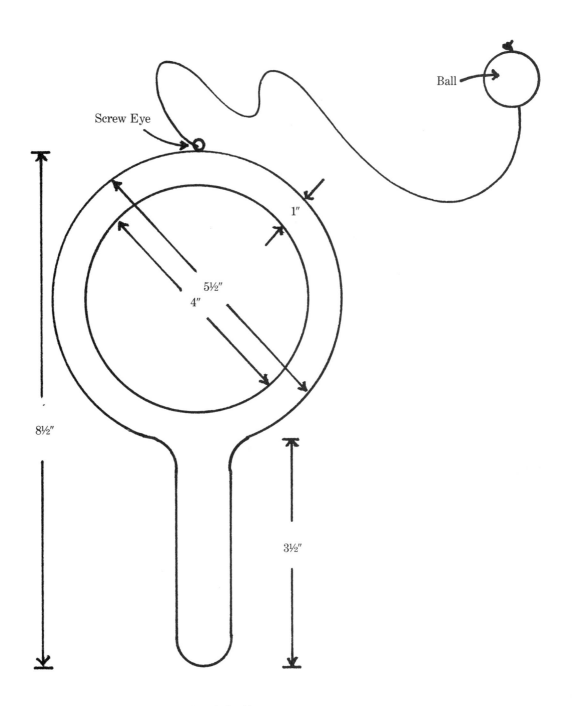

Ball

Screw Eye

1″

5½″

4″

8½″

3½″

Illus. 135.   Ball Through the Hole diagram

Top

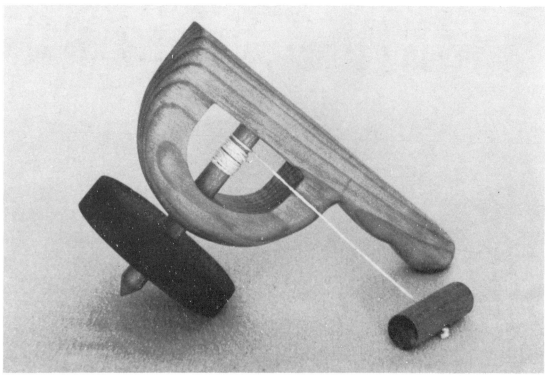

Illus. 136.

CUTTING LIST

Handle	1	*8″ × 3½″ × 1″*
Top	1	*3″ diam. circle*
Shaft	1	*½″ diam. dowel × 5″ long*
String		
Handle	1	*½″ diam. dowel × 2″ long*

You will also need: *a piece of string 15″ long.*

INSTRUCTIONS

1. Cut the handle to shape (see Illus. 137).
2. Drill a ⁹⁄₁₆″ diameter hole 3″ in to the handle piece from the bottom.
3. Cut out the center section.
4. Round off all edges using a ¼″ corner rounding bit on the router or sand well.
5. Sand and finish the handle.
6. Shape one end of the 5″-long dowel to a centered point.
7. Drill a small hole through the midpoint of the dowel big enough to accommodate the diameter of the pull string.
8. Drill a ½″ diameter hole through the center of the 3″ circle and insert the dowel shaft 1″ above the pointed end to make the top, using glue to secure it if necessary.
9. Sand Top smooth and finish. Painting a pattern on it makes it more interesting to watch as it spins.
10. Drill a narrow hole in the string handle to fit the string through.

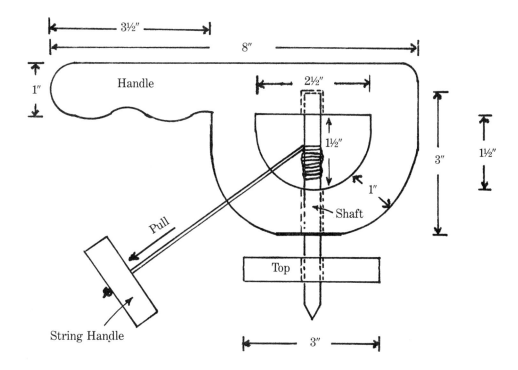

3½"

8"

Handle

1"

2½"

1½"

3"

1½"

1"

Shaft

Pull

String Handle

Top

3"

Illus. 137.   Top diagram

11. Sand well and finish.
12. Feed the string through the hole and tie a knot to hold it in place.

To set the Top spinning, insert the dowel up through the hole in the handle. Put the end of the string through the hole in the dowel and turn the spinning part by hand to wind the string around the dowel. Hold the handle with one hand, and with the point of the Top on the floor, pull the string with the other. Lift the handle clear of the Top and watch it spin.

Tic Tac Toe

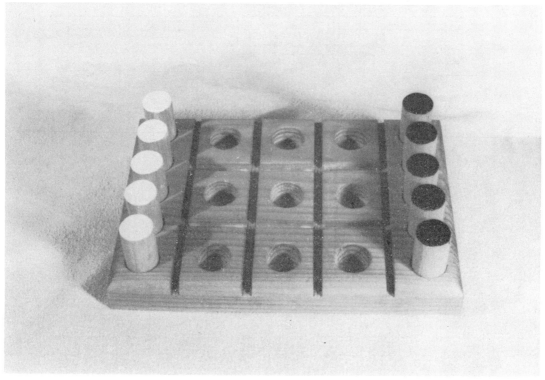

Illus. 138.

CUTTING LIST

Base	*1*	*11″ × 7¹/₁₆″ × 1″*
Dowel Pegs	*10*	*¾″ diam. cut to 2″ lengths*

INSTRUCTIONS

1. Cut base to finished size from 1″ stock as per Illus. 139.
2. Cut the dadoes ¼″ deep.
3. Finish the upper edges by adding a bevel, or use a router and ¼″ corner rounding or cove bit.
4. Drill the holes ¾″ deep. The holes are all ¹³/₁₆″ in diameter to loosely accommodate ¾″ dowel.
5. Sand and finish as desired.
6. Cut the pegs to correct length.
7. Sand the pegs well.
8. Finish with one of 4 methods. First, leave 5 of them natural and stain the other 5. Or, paint 5 of them one color and 5 a contrasting color. You can paint the whole peg or simply the top of each one. Thirdly, you can put an "X" on the ends of 5 using a saw to make a shallow kerf. A spur bit used to a shallow depth will give you "O"s. Lastly, paint "X"s and "O"s on them.

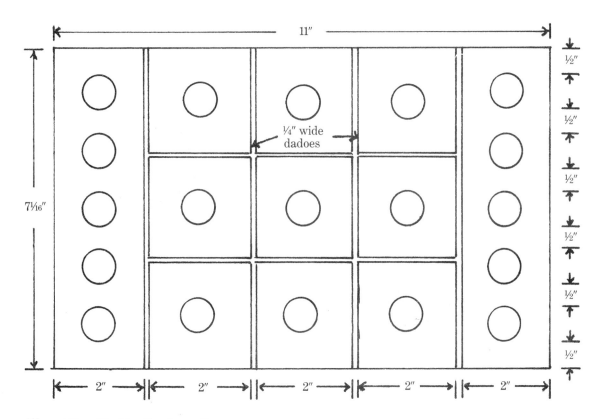

Illus. 139. Tic Tac Toe base diagram

Word Search

Illus. 140.

CUTTING LIST

Pentagons	*3*	*1½" thick and 1½" per side*
Dowel	*1*	*Approx. ¼" diam. × 5" long*
Wooden Beads	*2*	

INSTRUCTIONS

1. Drill a hole through the center of each pentagon to loosely accommodate the dowel. The diameter of the dowel will depend on the diameter of the beads you attach at each end.

2. Sand pentagons well and finish as desired.

3. Put letters on succeeding faces as follows. Left pentagon: b, d, r, s, m. Middle pentagon: a, e, i, o, u. Right pentagon: g, t, d, n, w.

4. Glue a bead to one end of the dowel. Insert the dowel through the pentagons and glue on the second bead.

5. Now see how many words you can find!

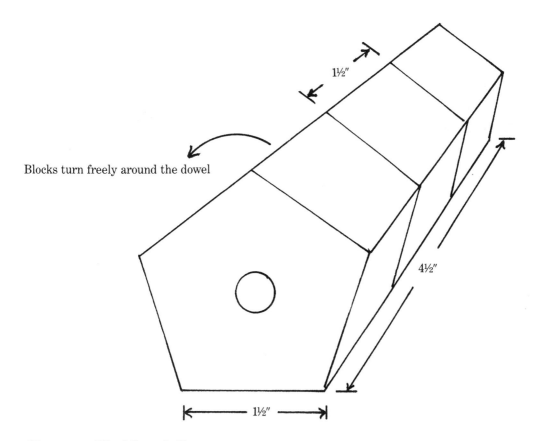

Blocks turn freely around the dowel

1½"

4½"

1½"

Illus. 141.   Word Search diagram

102

INDOOR PLAY

Building Blocks

Illus. 142.

Building Blocks provide hours of creative play for a wide range of age groups. They are great for using up those small pieces of wood lying around the shop. I bought a metal tool box to store them in which has proved very durable. You can also use a heavy cardboard box for storage and simply replace it as the need arises. A third option is to make a wooden storage box.

CUTTING LIST

6 blocks at 3" × 1½" × 1½"
11 blocks at 6" × 1½" × 1½"
   (6 remain at these dimensions and 5 are cut as per Illus. 143, 144 and 145)
9 blocks at 6" × 3" × 1½"
   (4 remain at these dimensions and 5 are cut as per Illus. 146, 147 and 148)
8 blocks at 3" × 3" × 1½"
   (4 remain at these dimensions and 4 are cut as per Illus. 149 and 150)
4 blocks at 3" × 1½" × ¾"
4 blocks at 6" × 1½" × ¾"
12 pieces of 1" diam. dowel
   (3 cut to 1½" lengths, 3 cut to 3" lengths, and 3 cut to 6" lengths)

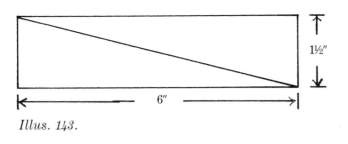

Illus. 143.

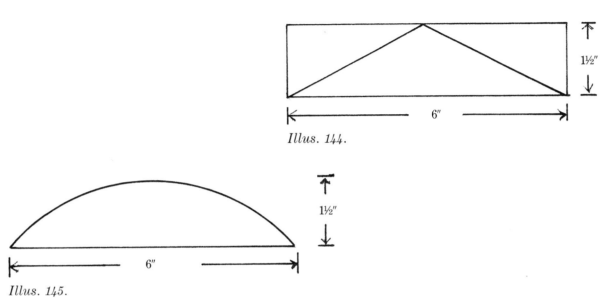

Illus. 144.

Illus. 145.

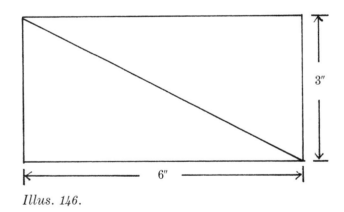

Illus. 146.

INSTRUCTIONS

1. Select 1½″ thick stock. Using different woods such as pine, mahogany and maple makes an attractive set.
2. Cut out each shape as per the cutting list and Illus. 143–150.
3. Sand all sides, and round all edges.
4. Finish as desired.

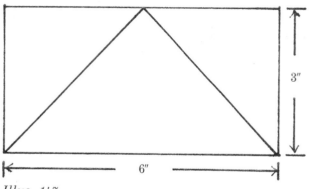

Illus. 147.

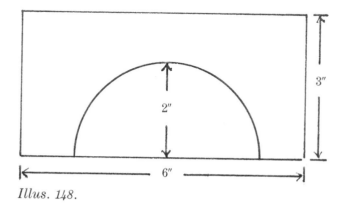

Illus. 148.

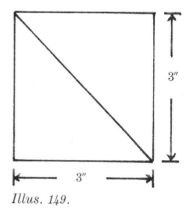

Illus. 149.

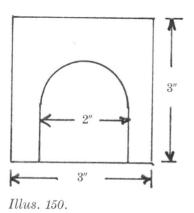

Illus. 150.

Art Easel/Blackboard

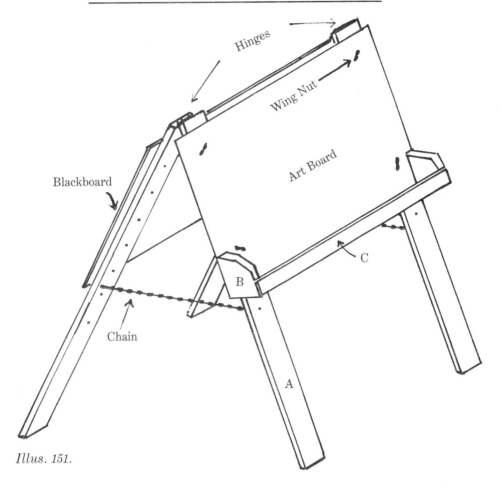

Hinges

Wing Nut

Art Board

Blackboard

C

B

Chain

A

Illus. 151.

A blackboard and easel combination provides two activity areas in a small space. The adjustable height will provide years of comfortable use as your artists grow. Buy your blackboard first, as its size will determine the spacing of the legs and you may want to cut the art easel to the same size. For this reason I have not included dimensions for the easel's painting surface.

CUTTING LIST

Legs A	*4*	*48" × 2½" × ¾"*
Shelf Ends B	*2*	*4" × 4" × ¾"*
Shelf Edge C	*1*	*2" × ¼" cut to suitable length*
Shelf D	*1*	*4" × ¾" cut to suitable length*
Art Board	*1*	*¼" stock cut to suitable size*
Blackboard	*1*	

You will also need: *4 screw eyes, eight 1½" × ¼" bolts, 8 wing nuts, 2 hinges, 2 pieces of chain about 18" long, some paint cups, glue and screws.*

INSTRUCTIONS

1. Cut 4 legs (A) to finished size (see Illus. 152).
2. Drill the holes in the legs to loosely accommodate a ¼″ bolt. Space the holes 3″ apart.
3. Sand the faces and any sharp edges. A corner rounding bit on a router makes a nice job of the edges.
4. Drill the holes for the hinges at the top of each pair of legs and for the screw eyes part way down the legs. Paint the legs or finish as desired.
5. Attach the hinges and screw eyes.
6. Cut the art board from ¼″ hardboard or other suitable material.
7. Cut all other pieces to finished size and shape (Illus. 153).
8. Cut the cup holes in the shelf (D) (Illus. 154). The size will be determined by the size of cup you use for your paints, pencils or brushes, so purchase these first. Inexpensive plastic cups can be purchased at most grocery stores.
9. Glue and screw the shelf ends (B) in place. Then install the shelf (D) and the front edge for the shelf (C).
10. Drill 4 holes 2″ in from each edge of the art board to loosely accommodate ¼″ bolts or wing nuts. Since the holes in the legs are 3″ apart, the holes in the art board should be 9″, 12″, 15″ or 18″ apart vertically—a multiple of three.
11. Finish as desired.
12. Drill 4 holes 2″ in from each edge of the blackboard to loosely accommodate ¼″ bolts or wing nuts, or simply screw the blackboard on to the legs in a permanent position.
13. Feed four ¼″ × 1½″ bolts through the legs and through the holes in the art board. Secure with wing nuts.
14. Repeat this procedure on the other side for the blackboard.
15. Mount the 18″ pieces of chain in the screw eyes (see Illus. 151).

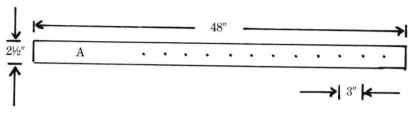

Illus. 152.   Art Easel legs

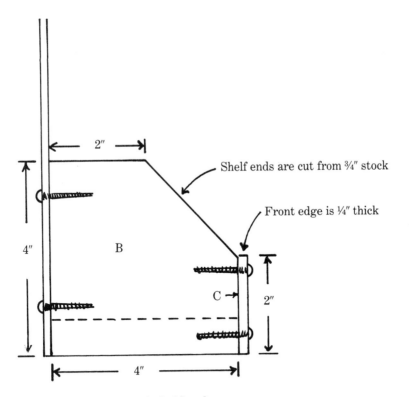

Shelf ends are cut from ¾″ stock

Front edge is ¼″ thick

Illus. 153.   *Art Easel shelf ends*

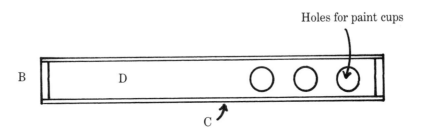

Holes for paint cups

Illus. 154.   *Art Easel shelf, top view*

Indoor Play Center

Illus. 155.

I designed the Play Center with long-term use in mind, thus the top (D) is indented to provide head room for a large person sitting and working at the desk as shown in Illus. 157. If you plan to use this only for young children, the top can be left as a rectangle and the upper deck area will be larger. The photo shows the Toy Boxes/Seats in place under the desk.

The "puppet theatre/closet" has holes drilled on each side for adjustable shelving.

When your children outgrow puppet shows, shelves can easily be added and the space used for storage.

The backing is not glued in place, only secured with screws for easy removal. As your child's tastes change the back can be repainted, repapered or refinished in other ways. The same refinishing can be done with the Toy Boxes/Seats.

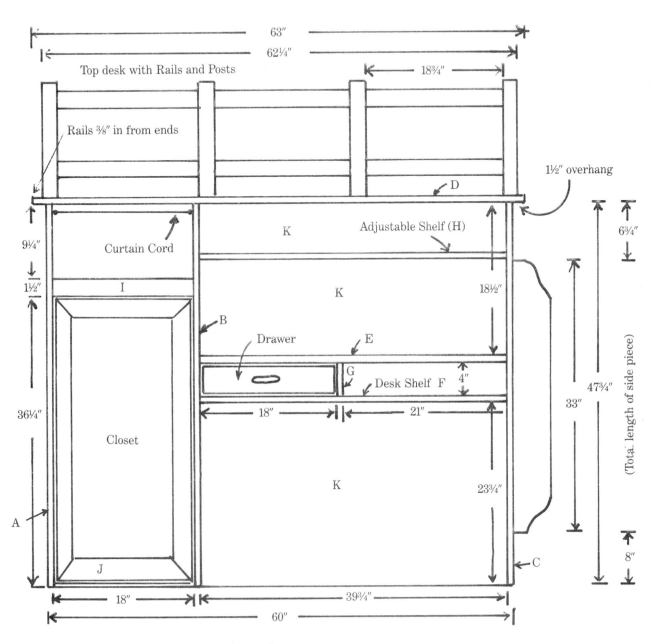

63"

62¼"

Top desk with Rails and Posts

18¾"

Rails ⅜" in from ends

1½" overhang

D

Curtain Cord

9¼"

K

Adjustable Shelf (H)

6¾"

1½"

I

K

18½"

B

Drawer

E

47¾" (Total length of side piece)

G

33"

Desk Shelf F

4"

18"

21"

36¼"

Closet

K

23¾"

A

J

C

8"

18"

39¾"

60"

Illus. 156.   Indoor Play Center, front view

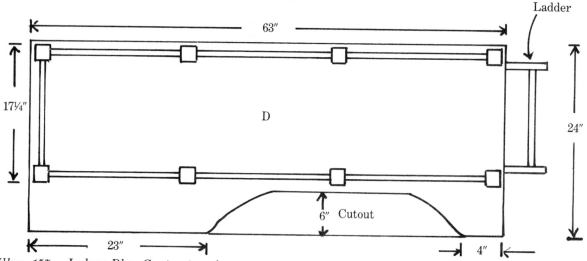

Illus. 157. Indoor Play Center, top view

MAIN BODY CUTTING LIST

Side A	*47¾" × 24" × ¾"*
Center Divider B	*47¾" × 24" × ¾"*
Side C	*47¾" × 24" ¾"*
Top D	*63" × 24" × ¾"*
Desk Top E	*40½" × 24" × ¾"*
Desk Shelf F	*40½" × 24" × ¾"*
Shelf Divider G	*4¾" × 24" × ¾"*
Adjustable Shelf H	*39⅝" × 10" × ¾"*
Crosspiece above	
* Door I*	*18" × 1½" × ¾"*
Closet Floor J	*24" × 18¾" × ¾"*
Backing K	*59" × 47⅞" × ¼"*

You will also need: *a door stop, veneer to finish the plywood edges, glue and #8 × 1½" screws.*

INSTRUCTIONS

1. Cut all pieces to their finished size and shape (refer to Illus. 156 and 157).
2. Cut a rabbet ½" wide on the back inside edge of the sides, bottom and top to accept the ¼" backing. Or, after you have assembled the Play Center, you can cut this rabbet with a router.
3. Cut the dadoes ⅜" deep for the desk and shelf in center divider (B) and side (C).
4. Cut the dadoes ⅜" deep in the under side of the top (D) for parts A, B and C to fit into.
5. Cut the dadoes in E and F ⅜" deep for the shelf divider (G).
6. Cut the rabbets ⅜" deep in the bottom inside edges of (A) and (B) to accept the closet floor.
7. Drill the holes for adjustable shelving on the inside surfaces of pieces A and B. Space them 4" apart vertically and 4" from each edge. Also drill the holes for the adjustable shelf on the inside surfaces of B and C. Space these 2" apart vertically: one row 2" from the back edge, the other row 9" from the back edge.
8. Using glue and screws assemble pieces (A) and (B) with the closet floor (J) and top (D), then add side (C), desk top (E), lower desk shelf (F), and shelf divider (G).
9. Using butt joints and finishing nails attach the crosspiece (I) which goes above the closet door.
10. Glue in a strip of wood to act as a door stop.

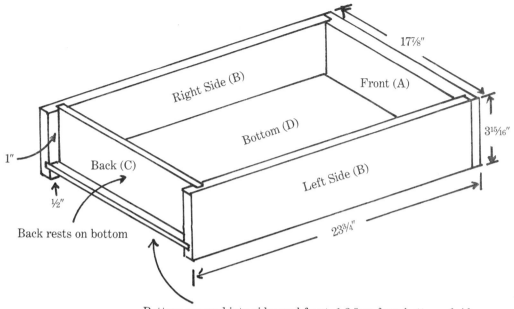

Right Side (B)

Front (A)

17⅞"

Bottom (D)

3¹⁵/₁₆"

1"

Back (C)

Left Side (B)

½"

Back rests on bottom

23¾"

Bottom grooved into sides and front, 1-2 " up from bottom of sides

Illus. 158. Drawer diagram

11. Finish all exposed edges with veneer strips.
12. Finish as desired after you add the door, ladder and top rail.
13. Finish the backing and screw it in place.

DRAWER CUTTING LIST

Front A	*1*	*17⅞" × 3¹⁵/₁₆" × ¾"*
Side B	*2*	*23⅜" × 3¹⁵/₁₆" × ½"*
Back C	*1*	*17⅜" × 3³/₁₆" × ½"*
Bottom D	*1*	*23¼" × 17⅜" × ¼"*

INSTRUCTIONS

1. Cut all the pieces to finished size (see Illus. 158).
2. Cut the dadoes ⁵/₁₆" wide and ¼" deep in the front (A) and sides (B) to fit the drawer bottom (D).
3. Cut the dadoes ½" wide and ¼" deep in the sides (B) to accept the back (C).
4. Cut the rabbets ½" wide and ⅜" deep on each side on the front (A).
5. Drill any necessary holes for the drawer handle in the front piece.
6. Assemble the four sides, then slide the bottom in place and secure it with a small set nail.

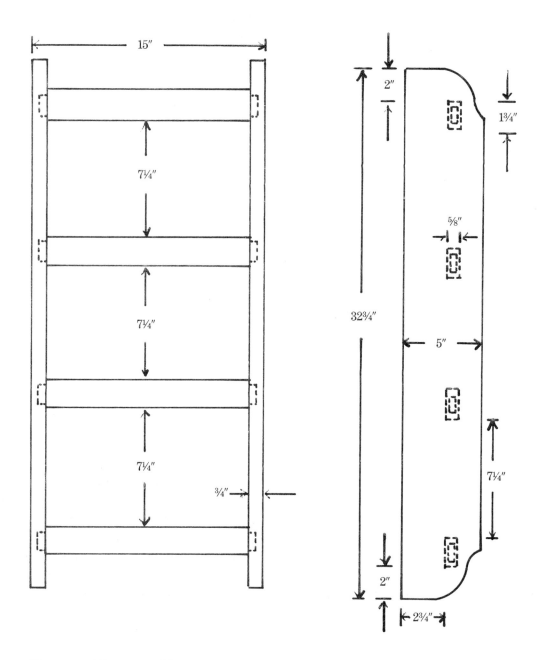

Illus. 159. Diagrams of front view of ladder (left) and side view of ladder (right)

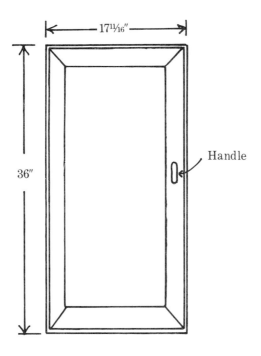

Illus. 160. Closet door diagram

LADDER CUTTING LIST

Sides	*2*	*32¾″ × 5″ × ¾″*
Rungs	*4*	*14½″ × 1¾″ × ⅝″*

INSTRUCTIONS

1. Cut all pieces to their finished size and shape (Illus. 159).
2. Cut mortise and tenon joints in the sides and on the ends of the rungs. Make the tenons ½″ long.
3. Assemble the ladder using a good quality glue.
4. Glue and screw the ladder from the inside to either end of the Play Center—the position of the Play Center in the room will determine which end you mount the ladder on.

DOOR

The door will be 36″ high × 17¹¹⁄₁₆″ wide. You can cut the door from one piece of ¾″ plywood and finish the exposed plywood edges, or you can make a door frame of ¾″ × 3″ stock using either butt joints or mitred corners. If you choose this method, rabbet the back inside edge and mount cork with a hardboard backing or a contrasting wood in the center part of the door. For either type of door, drill any necessary holes for the door handles and hinges. Use continuous hinge to mount the door.

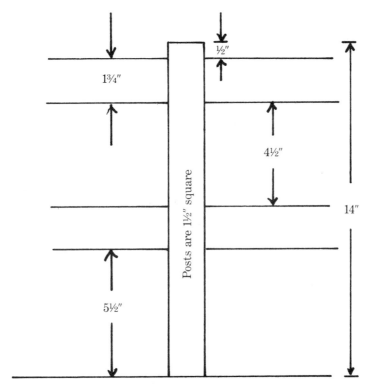

Illus. 161. Detail of top rail spacing

TOP RAILS AND POSTS CUTTING LIST

Posts	*8*	*14″ × 1½″ × 1½″*
Side Rails	*12*	*19¹³/₁₆″ × 1¾″ × ⅝″*
End Rails	*2*	*15¼″ × 1¾″ × ⅝″*

INSTRUCTIONS

1. Cut all pieces to their finished size (refer to Illus. 161).
2. Cut the mortise and tenon joints in the posts and rails. Cut the tenons ½″ long.
3. Router the edges and top of the posts with a ¼″ cove bit.
4. Router the edges of the rails with a ¼″ corner rounding bit.
5. Using glue, assemble the railing unit.
6. Place the railing on top of the play center accurately; mark hole sites to anchor the posts to the top. Drill the holes to accommodate ¼″ × 3″ lag bolts up through the top, then into the bottom of the posts. Countersink the heads of the bolts in a 1″ diameter hole so you have room to tighten the bolts with a socket wrench.

TOY BOXES/SEATS

The toy boxes are used as storage space and as seats for working at the desk. Since they are used as seats, you may wish to add foam rubber and upholstery to the lids. The sides can be finished to match the backing of the PlayCenter (I used the same wallpaper for both).

CUTTING LIST FOR ONE BOX

Sides	*2*	*17½" × 17" × ¼"*
Front	*1*	*18" × 17" × ¼"*
Back	*1*	*18" × 17½" × ¼"*
Bottom	*1*	*17¾" × 17¾" × ¾"*
Vertical Reinforcing Strips for Side	*4*	*13¼ × 1½" × ¾"*
Horizontal Reinforcing Strips for Side	*2*	*16" × 1½" × ¾"*
Horizontal Reinforcing Strip along Front	*1*	*17½" × 1½" × ¾"*
Horizontal Reinforcing Strip along Back	*1*	*17½" × 2" × ¾"*
Lid	*1*	*18½" × 18¼" × ½"*
Dowel	*2*	*½" diam. × 1½" long*

You will also need: *four ½" screw mounted casters, glue, screws, lid hinge, handle, two screw eyes and 18" of chain.*

INSTRUCTIONS

1. Cut all pieces to their finished size (Illus. 162 and 163). Note that the back is ½" taller than the front and sides — this combined with the dowels placed in the front edge will create a gap around the top edge to prevent fingers from getting pinched by a falling lid.
2. Attach three reinforcing strips—down each side and across the top—on the front and back. Dry clamp all four sides first to ensure proper placement of these strips.
3. Assemble the four sides to make a box.
4. Attach the reinforcing strips along the top edge of the sides.
5. Attach the bottom, recessing it 1½" from the bottom edge. This will fit 1½" casters.

If you use a different size of caster you may have to adjust the amount of recess.
6. Drill the holes for the dowel in the top front edge 1" deep and glue the dowel in place.
7. Finish as desired.
8. Hinge the top in place.
9. Add the screw eyes and chain to hold the lid in the open position.

ASSEMBLY

After you complete all the segments of the PlayCenter apply the desired finish or finishes and add handles and hinges. Since the PlayCenter is fairly large I recommend you attach the top railing after you have moved the PlayCenter to the room you want it in. Add a curtain across the puppet theatre.

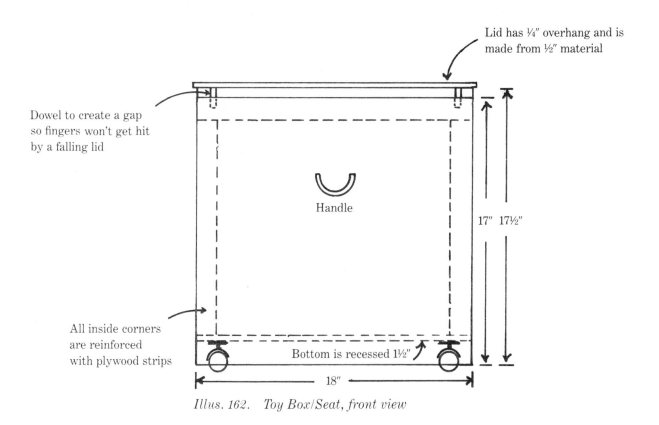

Lid has ¼″ overhang and is made from ½″ material

Dowel to create a gap so fingers won't get hit by a falling lid

Handle

17″ 17½″

All inside corners are reinforced with plywood strips

Bottom is recessed 1½″

18″

Illus. 162.   Toy Box/Seat, front view

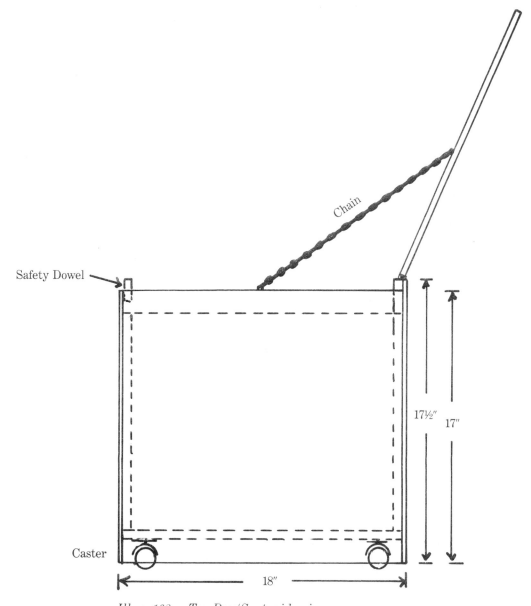

Illus. 163.   Toy Box/Seat, side view

TOY STORAGE

Under-the-Bed Storage Units

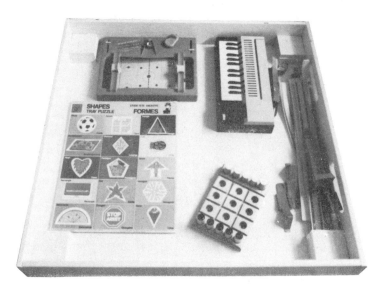

Illus. 164.

A simple box on casters allows you to utilize the space under the bed and gives quick and easy access to toys. The large area these storage units provide makes a great place to store large puzzles and race-car tracks. The casters are recessed for maximum vertical space. Two units can be placed under a twin bed.

CUTTING LIST

Side A	*2*	*34" × 5" × ¾"*
Side B	*2*	*32½" × 5" × ¾"*
Caster Enclosure C	*4*	*4¼" × 4¼" × ¾"*
Caster Enclosure D	*4*	*3½" × 1" × ¾"*
Caster Enclosure E	*4*	*4¼" × 1" × ¾"*
Bottom F	*1*	*34" × 34" × ¼"*

You will also need: *4 casters, screws and glue.*

INSTRUCTIONS

1. Cut all pieces to their finished size (refer to Illus. 164 and 165).
2. Cut the handholds on the two B sides to 6" long and 1½" wide.
3. Assemble the four sides using butt joints.
4. Cut the corners out of the bottom, then screw the bottom in place. Each cutout piece should be 4¼" × 4¼".
5. In each corner assemble the caster enclosure (Illus. 166). The enclosures are designed to accommodate a 1½" caster.
6. Sand and round off all sharp edges. Finish as desired.
7. Mount screw-type casters and roll away under the bed.

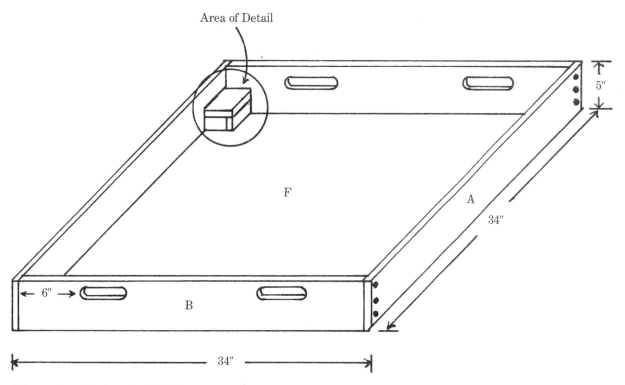

Area of Detail

5″

F

A

34″

6″

B

34″

Illus. 165. Under-the-Bed Storage Unit diagram

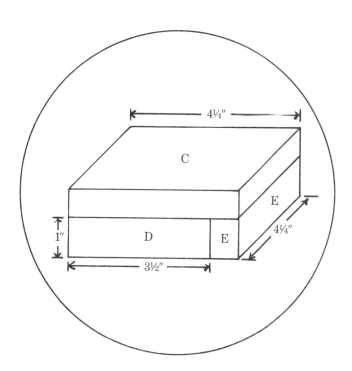

4¼″

C

E

1″

D

E

4¼″

3½″

Illus. 166. Detail of caster enclosure

Adjustable Toy Shelves

Illus. 167.

The shelves can be made with or without the sliding doors (the photo shows the shelf without the doors). The finish on the doors can be made to match the Indoor Play Center and seats. The kick has been recessed to allow the unit to be placed over a hot-air heating vent in case lack of floor space makes that necessary.

CUTTING LIST

Side A	*2*	*32" × 14¾" × ¾"*
Top Shelf B	*1*	*47¾" × 14¾" × ¾"*
Bottom Shelf C	*1*	*47¾" × 14½" × ¾"*
Adjustable Shelves D	*2*	*46¹⁵⁄₁₆" × 13½" × ¾"*
Back of Top Shelf E	*1*	*47" × 1" × ¾"*
Back F	*1*	*48" × 30¼" × ¼"*
Kick G	*1*	*47" × 3" × ¾"*

You will also need: *2 pieces for the sliding doors cut from ¼" material. They should be 24" wide and approximately 27" tall.*

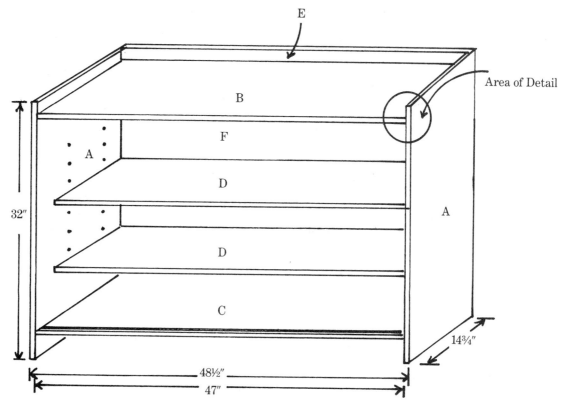

Illus. 168. Adjustable Toy Shelves, front view

INSTRUCTIONS

1. Cut all pieces to finished size (Illus. 168, 169 and 170).
2. Cut the dadoes ⅜" deep in the sides (A) to accommodate the top and bottom shelves.
3. Cut rabbets along the back edges of the sides (A) to accept the ¼" backing. The rabbets should be ½" wide.
4. Rabbet the front edges of the top and bottom shelves (B and C) to accept the sliding door tracks. The dimensions will be determined by the size of the track you use.
5. Drill the holes for the adjustable shelves (D). Holes for adjustable shelves are 2" from the back and 4" from the front on a 2" vertical spacing. The shelves can be supported by short pieces of dowel, or by plastic or metal shelf supports. The size of the holes you drill will be determined by which method of support you choose.
6. Assemble the sides (A) and top and bottom shelves (B and C). If you lay the backing (F) in place when you clamp the shelf it will help to keep it square. Add the kick (G) and the back of the top shelf (E) using butt joints.
7. Add the sliding door tracks, following the directions which come with the track.
8. Finish the exposed edges of the plywood and cover the sliding door tracks with strips of wood or veneer. Finish the front edges of the adjustable shelves as well.

9. The height of the doors must be measured after you install the door tracks, since this varies according to the track used. Cut the doors to their finished size and install finger pulls.
10. Finish as desired.
11. Screw the back (F) in place, drop the doors in their tracks, add the shelves and fill with toys.

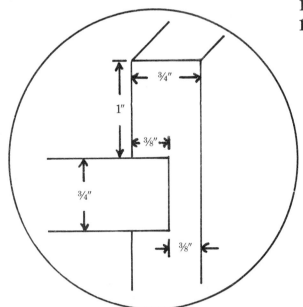

3/4"

1"

3/8"

3/4"

3/8"

Illus. 169. Detail of corner assembly, showing dado dimensions

14¾"

Backing only goes this high

Track for Doors

¼" Backing

13½"

Track for Doors

3"

9"

Kick (G)

Illus. 170. Adjustable Toy Shelves, end view

Index